"The spring breeze, faintly cool, blows and wakes me from my drunkenness, A faint chill in the air, and the slanted sunlight on the mountain peak greets me, I turn back and look at the desolate place I've passed, And return home - there is no wind, no rain, nor sunshine."

I0627039

Dedication

This book is dedicated to my dear husband Say Lau Chan Our oldest daughter Rosaline Chan and her family Our second daughter Christine Chan and her family Our son Eugene Chan and his family.

Foreword by Close Friends

We are honored to pen this foreword, introducing readers to the remarkable life story presented in this retrospective autobiography. It unveils the journey of a lady we knew intimately and proudly regarded as a best friend.

Our association spans nearly a year as close friends of Sim Bee Sian. During that time, as young girls, we dominated the basketball court together, advancing and retreating as one. It was then that we recognized her not only as an outstanding player but also as a resilient and industrious individual. She stood apart from ordinary women, confronting challenges with unwavering determination. Rather than retreating in the face of difficulty, she grew more courageous, persisting until success was achieved. Her unyielding perseverance became a guiding principle and a key factor in her career success.

Half a century ago, she embarked on an immigrant's journey to Canada, a tale that epitomizes the dreams of that era. Starting anew in a foreign land with no background or resources, she relied on her own efforts and talents to establish a thriving business. Her success wasn't a happenstance but the outcome of continuous learning and progress. Her story serves as an inspiration, particularly for those dreaming of making a living in a foreign country.

Despite living in Canada for five decades, she maintains a deep connection to her hometown, never forgetting her roots and staying in touch with relatives and friends back home. With boundless energy, she took up the cello and writing in her later years, embodying the spirit of "live until you are old and learn until you are old," truly amazing us.

This autobiography transcends a mere memoir; it is a textbook brimming with wisdom and inspiration, teaching us resilience in adversity, the pursuit of dreams, and the discovery of beauty in life. It imparts invaluable life lessons, inspiring the belief that with unwavering faith, any difficulty can be overcome.

We hope you relish this autobiography, and we extend our heartfelt wishes to our friend Bee Sian for continued success and happiness on her life's journey.

Best friends,

Phan Joon Fah, Chua Mui Ai, Wong Jee Chin, Lian Moi Moi, Lian Ching Mee and Ng Siew Phin

Forward from the Eldest Daughter

Standing at the watershed of time, I reflect upon the magical and wondrous journey of my mother's life with a heart full of gratitude and admiration. As her eldest daughter, I feel a profound responsibility to convey my innermost sentiments and share this invaluable autobiography, chronicling her early struggles, the establishment of our family, challenges and triumphs, passions and interests, and the profound love shared with others.

Recalling the past, vivid memories emerge of my mother orchestrating a grand birthday celebration for me and my siblings. Those scenes, brimming with laughter and beauty, remain the most cherished moments of my childhood. It was through these events that I felt her deep love for family and her unwavering pursuit of happiness. Despite her busy schedule, she provided us with the best resources and the support needed for our care and education.

Yet, beneath the surface, I also sensed the sacrifices she made, with very little time for personal interactions or a deeper understanding of her children's lives. Her love manifested not in physical intimacy but through her actions. Her strict expectations for us to remain positive and excel in everything influenced my values of hard work and the pursuit of success.

Despite Canada's distinct cultural background, she actively promotes Chinese culture, emphasizing family harmony and displaying a steadfast commitment to family traditions and rituals, such as celebrating the Chinese Spring Festival. This instills in us a deep appreciation for cultural heritage.

Her zest for life and love for learning shine through in her passion for gardening, transforming the yard and balcony of our home into vibrant sanctuaries amid her hectic work life.

Her life has been rife with challenges, yet she consistently overcomes them tenaciously, proving her mettle. Emerging from a relatively humble background, she achieved success through sheer hard work. I witnessed her dedication to her career and the joyous moments within our family, especially during the inauguration of the first store and the arrival of my younger brother. These are the fruits of her labor and the glorious milestones in her life.

Being my mother's eldest daughter fills me with deep pride and gratitude. Her life epitomizes resilience in the face of adversity and an unwavering commitment to overcoming rough times. She didn't rely on others but rather on her steadfast will and selfless dedication to gradually forge a new world. Her story inspires me to view life's challenges not as obstacles but as opportunities to sharpen our resolve.

May this book convey my mother's perseverance and determination, inspiring others to courageously tread their own paths in life. The river of maternal love never runs dry, and I am committed to perpetuating her tenacity and love, allowing the saga of this family to endure.

I send my mother my most sincerest regards, who has persevered through the years.

Rosaline

Forward from the Nephew

Dear Reader,

In my view, this autobiography presents an opportunity for me to introduce you to a truly special person in my life - my beloved aunt, Sim Bee Sian. Through this preface, I aim to offer background information on why this autobiography is a compelling read and provide you with my personal perspective.

My aunt has been an adult I've admired since my childhood. Her life in Canada is filled with stories and achievements celebrated among our relatives. As I grew older, I was fortunate enough to establish a close connection with her, being treated like her own child. I witnessed numerous milestones in her life, sharing in her joys and sorrows. Throughout this time, I gained a profound understanding of her tenacity, wisdom, courage, and unwavering determination in the face of life's ups and downs.

This autobiography serves as a testament to her growth, a narrative laden with hardships and a journey fraught with challenges and opportunities. From her early years to her current accomplishments, you will encounter a story of continuous pursuit of excellence and an indomitable spirit that refuses to surrender.

Her background, spanning from family life to entrepreneurial experiences, has molded her into the remarkable person she is today. One of the key values of this autobiography lies in its ability to convey a message about perseverance and the pursuit of dreams. Her story has not only inspired me but also countless others, instilling the belief that, no matter the odds, we can overcome them with strong faith and determination.

In her youth, my aunt displayed unwavering devotion to her large family, even sacrificing her studies to care for her younger siblings.

Her deep affection for family and independent spirit empowered her to confront challenges related to language, culture, and life, bravely embracing new opportunities upon immigrating to Canada.

In her tailoring career, Auntie demonstrated relentless effort and professionalism, achieving success not only in her professional endeavors but also in expanding her network with local individuals. She is not just a successful career woman but also a family-oriented mother who skillfully balances career and family through effective time management.

Studying in the West, my aunt integrated into Western culture while preserving the richness of Chinese heritage. Her fighting spirit, determination to confront challenges, and persistent belief in family and clan are all aspects worth reflecting upon in this autobiography. She cares deeply for her relatives, friends, and siblings, hoping that everyone will recognize the contributions of the Sim family's ancestors in the development of Long Lama. She does not want her true deeds to fade into the dust of history, and, believing in cause and effect, she diligently works to excel in everything she does.

This book unveils that she is not merely a participant in life but also a thinker and inspirer. Witness how she employs her story to motivate and inspire others. Her narrative teaches us that every moment in life holds value and everyone possesses the ability to shape their own destiny.

Therefore, dear reader, I wholeheartedly recommend investing your time in reading this autobiography. Within its pages, you'll discover the transformative power of courage, hope, and resilience that will inspire you to pursue your dreams, regardless of the difficulties you may face. Her story unfolds as a genuine and profound life journey marked by challenges and wonders, and I am confident that you will derive significant benefits from it.

May you find inspiration, feel hope, and realize your capacity to create a life imbued with meaning.

Sincerest wishes,
Nephew Sim Chin Yan

My Life Journey

Table of Contents

Preface

Life unfolds uniquely over the span of seventy years. Much of my journey has been spent contemplating the relentlessness of time. Yet, I resonate deeply with Zhu Ziqing's sentiment: "But the sunset is infinitely beautiful, so why be melancholy near dusk." I refuse to be confined by the years. Despite entering my twilight years, I perceive life as luminous, soft, and warmly comforting.

If life is a book, my intention is to transcribe it into words. This book serves as a representation of my heart. Each page within this life narrative encapsulates the ebb and flow of accomplishments and losses, the realization of dreams and regrets, and the overlay of happiness and sadness. To peruse these pages is to step into my world, into my heart. Welcome!

This memoir has taken nearly two years—from gathering information to dictating and organizing. It predominantly commemorates family and friends, delving into the journey of relocating to Canada, entrepreneurial endeavors, the battle against illness, and personal experiences and insights.

My heartfelt intention is to convey sentiments to future generations. I wish to articulate every concealed fragment of my past, hidden in the recesses of my heart, into sentences, allowing them to comprehend their parents' struggles and fathom the origins of their own lives. With this aspiration, I embarked on the journey of publishing this memoir. If it serves to inspire future generations, that would be fulfillment enough!

My life journey can be delineated into three distinct stages. The first, the teenage stage, transpired before immigrating to Canada, during the period in Miri, living under the same roof with my parents, brothers, and sisters. Notably, due to objective circumstances, I formed connections with a group of basketball teammates who shared my experiences, and together, we fought side by side to triumph in the game.

The second stage unfolded after immigrating to Canada with my husband, encompassing a severe car accident, venturing into tailoring business, real estate investments, and involvement in direct sales. From academic pursuits to entrepreneurial endeavors, I was fortunate to receive support from various quarters, establishing a solid foundation locally and gaining a profound understanding of interpersonal relationships. Sincere treatment of one another is invaluable.

The third stage involves an enlightened understanding of life following a battle with cancer and subsequent recovery. Throughout, I have maintained an optimistic and resilient disposition, endeavoring diligently each day.

Reflecting on my journey, I express gratitude to Dr. Brian Fernandes. Without him as a compassionate and competent doctor, my present state would not have been possible. His kindness and apt prescriptions alleviated my pain, restoring my health. I also extend thanks to my godmother, Mrs. Byrne Hindley, for her encouragement and support during times of illness, preventing discouragement. Additionally, I appreciate the Malaysian artist Jun Yi. Being part of his fan circle has injected vitality and music into my current life. His encouragement emboldens me to explore new horizons.

For the creation of this book, I revisited my hometown of Miri multiple times. I enlisted the expertise of Chua Yong Chee, a seasoned local media professional with over 20 years in the newspaper industry, to pen and organize my memoirs. During this process, I reconnected with relatives and friends. Time has brought change, and those once brimming with youth and vitality have transformed into gray-haired grandparents.

In conclusion, I extend gratitude once again to author Chua Yong Chee for patiently listening to my dictation before crafting the narrative in this book. Simultaneously, heartfelt thanks go to editorial board member Pauline Yong Bee Hie for meticulous editing and reviewing, ensuring the timely completion of this book.

Chapter 1
A Timeless Bond

In the vibrant year of 1968, a spirited group of young girls united by their love for basketball formed the formidable Xieyuan team. Among them, a lasting friendship blossomed between me and Sim Bee Sian, my best friend. Our ambitious endeavors took us to various corners, engaging in friendly basketball matches, acquiring experiences, and fostering camaraderie. A pinnacle achievement remains etched in our memories—the Miri District Three-Year Basketball Challenge Champions Cup, where Captain Phan Joon Fah represented Sarawak in the Heads of State Championship Basketball Tournament, securing third place.

As the years passed, life unfolded, and the once basketball-enthralled teammates embraced new roles in the journey of marriage and family. Sim Bee Sian and Chen Sui Ching, now settled in Canada, Captain Phan Joon Fah residing in Sibu, we ventured through the tapestry of fifty-three years. Occasional reunions with the Miri District team became the sole rendezvous for our scattered paths.

Last year, on November 12, 2022, Bee Sian's return from Canada marked her 70th birthday celebration. Chua Mui Ai's initiative brought us together, orchestrating a collective cake-cutting ceremony, weaving a tapestry of joy and warmth. Time is a relentless river, but on July 16, 2023, we reconvened in Sibu to celebrate our 71st birthday. Our bond strengthened, and our camaraderie deepened. Gratitude filled our hearts, especially towards Bee Sian, whose arrangements bestowed upon us these precious moments.

In our embrace of old age, our spirits remain ageless. Mui Ai, endearingly known as Pistachio, graces our gatherings with her beauty, humor, and summoning prowess, connecting us with her contagious enthusiasm. Phang Ma Qun, a talented singer in our midst, once claimed victory in the Miri District Singing Competition wit h the soul-stirring "In Spring."

Our dear friend, Sim Bee Sian, stands as a testament to resilience, warmth, and generosity. Her Canadian sojourn reflects a life of hard work, starting anew, and triumphing over adversities. Her harmonious family radiates love, filial piety, and wisdom through generations. She meticulously recorded her life experiences, crafting a personal autobiography to inspire future generations —an exquisite testament to the essence of beauty.

To Fairy, we extend wishes for perpetual fam ily happiness, safety, health, and auspiciousness. As teammates, we share some "good words": live healthily, stay reasonably busy, embrace life to the fullest, and cherish happy gatherings.

Destined by shared glory on the basketball court, we cherish our sincere friendship, wishing it a long and prosperous life.

Chapter 2
Roots of Resilience

I came into this world in 1952 amid the serene landscapes of Long Lama, a quaint mountain town nestled along the Baram River in Miri Province, Sarawak. A town that was, at that time, a tapestry of indigenous communities—primarily Kayan, Kenyan, and Penan—with only a sprinkling of Chinese settlers. Long Lama, now the county seat of Telang Usan District, evolved from a humble port into a thriving hub. The completion of the Long Lama Bridge in 2019 erased ferry service constraints, ushering in a new era of accessibility and development. Today's Long Lama, unlike the arid hamlet of my youth, stands transformed.

My grandfather, Sim Chen Luk, a Fujian native, migrated to Sarawak and made Long Lama his home. The port's inception in 1905 marked the beginning of trade, with my grandfather partnering with Lee Kai Tai to establish "Xinhe'an Company." Trading with local indigenous people for bamboo, rattan, and rice, they operated from the opposite shore before relocating. By 1927, nine wooden shops adorned the landscape, and a burgeoning Chinese community shaped the town.

My father, Sim Peng Kok, born in 1904, studied in China, shuttling between Sarawak and his homeland. After marrying my mother, Mujan Jau, they settled in Long Lama. From this union came 11 children, with my father's teachings resonating in every facet of our lives. Growing up in Long Lama was a cacophony of family, laughter, and shared experiences. Our crowded home, brimming with siblings, was a testament to love and togetherness.

Nostalgia takes me back to our primary school days at Kee Tee Primary School, founded on land donated by my father. Among my siblings, my second brother and I formed an unbreakable bond, especially during my teenage years when I moved to Miri to work. His guidance and mentorship shaped my journey.

Our parents, immersed in business and farming, toiled ceaselessly for our well-being. From running a floating grocery store to managing a rubber plantation, my father epitomized versatility. A skilled traditional Chinese medicine practitioner, he treated villagers with affability, patience, and gentleness. My mother, a diligent Kayan woman, managed our household with boundless kindness. She adapted to Chinese cuisine for my father and assumed the role of a nurturing matriarch.

My early years were marked by dawn visits to the rubber plantation with my father, followed by cooking over an open fire and processing rubber. My father's repertoire included skills beyond farming; he was a traditional Chinese doctor, often treating villagers with herbal remedies.

The richness of my parents' teachings became apparent as I navigated life's challenges. Immigrating to Canada at 21, I cherished each visit home but felt the ticking clock of fleeting time. A deep regret lingered

I couldn't spend enough days serving my parents as filial piety demanded. Yet, a pivotal moment came when, for my father's 80th birthday, children and grandchildren gathered, enveloping him in familial joy. His eventual passing in 1986 and my mother's stroke-ridden final years were poignant chapters.

In 2014, I returned from Canada to Miri, joining my siblings to build graves and monuments for our parents. As I stood before the tombstone, engraved with their names and life's timeline, a flood of nostalgia and gratitude overwhelmed me. My parents, who gave me life, raised me and instilled resilience, deserved everlasting gratitude. Their legacy lives on in my heart.

"Longing for my hometown, thinking of my parents' love and kindness."

"The posthumous photograph of my late father, Sim Peng Kok."

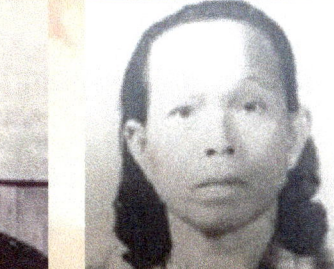

"The posthumous photograph of my late mother, Mujan Jau."

"On July 22, 2023, I returned to the old house located in Long Lama, which holds all of my childhood memories. The one in blue is my second sister, Bee Ching, and the one in yellow is my youngest sister, Bee Hiang."

"I am offering prayers at the temple in my hometown of Long Lama."

☒ The gravestone of my late father, Sim Bing Kok."
☒ "The gravestone of my late mother, Mujan Jau."

"In my hometown of Long Lama, I joyfully reunite with relatives and friends."

Chapter 3
A Letter to My Beloved Parents

Dear Parents,

As time dances on the wings of fleeting years, I find myself in a realm of boundless longing, crafting a paper crane with hopes that it will ascend into the skies, traversing myriad mountains and rivers to convey the depth of my thoughts to you.

Thank you for gifting me life, enabling me to frolic in this beautiful and vibrant world, experiencing the profound tapestry of existence. It is through your unwavering toil that I comprehend the true value of life; your meticulous guidance is etched indelibly in my heart. Your noble character has become the lodestar I incessantly strive to emulate, and your selfless love, an enduring beacon illuminating my path.

In this foreign land where I currently reside, I fold the yesterdays you bestowed upon me into a vessel of memory, allowing it to sail upon the vast ocean of yearning. Gratitude fills my heart for granting me the chance to pursue happiness and comprehend its essence. You, my guides through life's journey, have taught me the art of gratitude and the essence of being a virtuous individual.

Life's symphony led me to encounter the most refined version of myself at the most opportune age. Gratitude extends to my relatives for their boundless care, allowing me to taste the sweetness of familial affection. To the teachers, whose meticulous teachings immersed me in the ocean of knowledge, and to friends whose unwavering support helped me surmount myriad challenges—I am profoundly thankful.

Parents, you gifted me the ruler of life, enabling me to measure every stride forward; you presented a mirror of example, reflecting the radiance of diligence, perseverance, and love. From the depths of my heart, I express my gratitude. It is your nurturing and guidance that have fostered my growth. In times of distress, you stand beside me; in moments of despondency, you ignite the flame of hope; in times of struggle, you are the unwavering cheerleader.

Dear parents, I yearn to share my joys and triumphs with you. Alas, you exist only in the realms of dreams, where our souls intertwine.

In humble reverence, I aspire to emulate the grass, grateful to the silent earth. Your pure paternal and maternal love shielded me from life's tempests, providing a nurturing field filled with love and warmth. On life's journey, I express gratitude for shielding me from adversities; in emotional pursuits, I appreciate your tolerance and understanding; on life's path, I am thankful for your tender care. On this day of gratitude, my deepest thanks I offer.

Living in a state of gratitude is true happiness. Your watchful gaze propels me forward on the road of life. Thank you for weathering storms by my side and uplifting me when I felt most powerless.

Dear parents, you reside eternally in the sanctum of my heart, and I yearn for you profoundly.

May gratitude forever grace my heart.

Your Eldest Daughter,
Sim Bee Sian

Chapter 4
Women's Basketball Warriors Long Live Friendship

Since the tender age of 13, I delved into the world of basketball, becoming part of the Long Lama Junior Girls Team alongside my cousin, Sim Eng Moi. Within the team, Wu Meijing and I, the youngest and boldest, earned the moniker "Little Peppers." At 15, Wu Meijing joined the Krokop District Xieyuan Women's Basketball Team in Miri, and together with a sisterhood of like-minded individuals, we embarked on numerous competitions, both grand and intimate.

Representing a renowned basketball team, our victories were almost a given in every game, including securing the championship in the inaugural Men's and Women's Basketball Open in Miri. Newspapers avidly covered our matches, and the popularity of our team was evident in the frequent appearances of our names and jersey numbers in print—mine being No. 5.

The 1960s marked our era, and at 17, I, along with teammates like Phan Joon Fah (captain), Wong Jee Chin, Chua Moi Ai, Lian Moi Moi, and others, exuded youthful vigor. The diversity in our personalities

lively, innocent, serious, smart, enthusiastic—did not hinder our camaraderie. Bound by our passion for basketball, we toiled diligently, even stitching our jerseys stitch by stitch.

Our captain, Phan Joon Fah, showcased a soft demeanor off-court but transformed into a stalwart backbone during games. Daily practices were rigorous, drenched in sweat, and marked by unwavering dedication. I, as a guard, would wake at 4 a.m., stumbling to Krokop Primary School's basketball court in the dark, honing my skills.

Our efforts bore fruit as we clinched three consecutive Miri District Challenge Cups, a source of immense pride. Beyond local triumphs, we ventured to Baram, Brunei, Sabah, and various Sarawak locales, fostering precious memories through friendly matches and exchange activities.

Traveling on a limited budget in 1969, sponsored by "Xie Yuan Welding Factory," led by Sim Shou Fook and coached by Qiu Xue Kui, we traversed Sarawak, Seria, Bandar Seri Begawan, and Labuan. Enduring meager accommodations, we bonded, becoming inseparable sisters.

Our synergy, unity, and trust in each other propelled us to victory. We showcased precision in passing, supporting, and attacking, effortlessly maneuvering past opponents. Our focus on team success over personal achievements defined our ethos, securing victory through passion and perseverance.

Coached by the tall, talented, and wise Qiu Xue Kui, our success, spanning five years (1966-1971), reflected both individual efforts and effective leadership. Although a loss to the Sibu team in 1971 was a setback, our legacy persisted as teammates were selected as Sarawak representatives.

Basketball wasn't merely a sport for us; it became a cornerstone of enduring friendships. Reuniting in 2023 at Wangxi House Restaurant in Sibu to celebrate birthdays, the camaraderie remained palpable. Through the passing years, our friendship endured, echoing the basketball beats eternally etched in our hearts.

In the tapestry of our memories, we remain the same spirited girls, relishing the echoes of youth. As time marches on, our friendship remains unwavering, akin to the everlasting melody of basketball resonating in our hearts. Cheers to our enduring camaraderie, a timeless anthem that transcends the years.

"The women's basketball warriors, long live friendship!"

"The basketball players display their agility and poise as they compete for the ball."

第一屆少年男女蘋球公開賽協源隊冠軍百幹聯合影

"The Xieyuan team, champions of the first Miri Youth Boys' and Girls' Basketball Open Tournament, take a group photo with the officials."

"Taken on the bus as we set off for the out-of-town competition."

On the way to a tournament

"A group photo of the Xieyuan girls' basketball team members."

Team picture at a basketball tournament in 1969
1969

"A group photo of the Xieyuan team members at the 1969 Basketball Championship."

1971 tournament champions
1971

"A group photo of the Xieyuan team members at the 1971 Basketball Championship."

"Former teammates and close sisters joyfully reunite."

"In our youthful beauty, we were also dressed very fashionably."

"Former teammates reunite in Sibu."

"Roaming freely in Sibu, enjoying the time together."

"The Xieyuan women's basketball teammates gathered at a restaurant in Sibu to celebrate a 71st birthday. From left to right:Lian Ching Mee, Sim Bee Sian, Lian Moi Moi, Chua Mui ai, Ng Siew Phin, and Phan Joon Fah."

Chapter 5
Beautiful Acquaintance and Cherishing Each Other

I met my love in 1971. When I met him, I had already started working as a domestic help in my boss's house. The workweek is six days, with Sundays off. Every Sunday, I would stay at my second brother's farm in Tukau District. The farm has about 6 acres of land and raises a lot of poultry. The most amazing thing is that it raises more than a thousand chickens and also has a pepper garden.

At that time, as the representative of Krokop District Xieyuan Women's Basketball Team, whenever my team played a game, there was one person who came to watch almost every game. He secretly paid attention to me for a period and knew something about me and where I worked. On the contrary, I did not know that such a person existed. Until one day, my boss's hot water heater broke down, and he asked the oil company to send someone to repair it. The man also took the opportunity to follow the repairman to the house, and this is how my relationship with him began.

Since then, this person has become more and more active. He started calling me frequently, but I didn't answer. He did not give up because of this and wrote three more letters to me and sent them to the boss's house. Then, he called me and asked me why I didn't reply. I said that we didn't know each other, so of course, I wouldn't reply to him. He was not discouraged. On the contrary, he became more and more courageous and tried every means to meet or say a word to me.

In such a stalemate, I asked close relatives and friends around me about this person's family background, character, and behavior. At the same time, I also consulted my respected second brother, who works in a grocery store and happens to know the other person's family. I learned from them that the family's surname was Chan, and they were family members who ran breakfast stalls (fried kway teow, selling

15

steamed buns), etc. Because I knew some information about his family, I felt a little at ease.

Later, when the other person came to see me again, I let down my guard and tried to date him. Just like that, the relationship between me and him was established!

After 5 to 6 months of dating, one day, my love told me that his application for a job in Canada had been approved, and he hoped that I would consider waiting for him to return to Malaysia before getting married. At that time, I was full of contradictions and did not agree with him easily. Since my boss is Canadian, he enthusiastically told us some Canadian customs and conditions. However, my boss also had selfish motives. He was afraid that when my love went abroad, he would definitely take me away with him, so he gradually became unwelcome for my love to visit me.

After dating for half a year, my love saw that the time was right and took me home to meet my parents. As soon as his family saw me, they asked me if I believed in Buddhism. I answered yes. They were cordial and happy. I felt accepted and immediately felt that it was suitable to continue our relationship with him. In order to ease the tension between my boss and my love, I quit my old job after thinking about it, found a new one, and planned to get engaged to my love.

As for my parents, at first, they were not in favor of me dating my love, but later, they agreed to our engagement. In the 1960s, there were not many people in the small town of Long Lama. My parents were engaged in business and farming, and the neighbors knew each other. Some people even asked matchmakers to come to their parents' homes to propose marriage to them, hoping that I would become their daughter-in-law. Rather than this unknown "outsider", my parents preferred that I marry a "local person" they were familiar with. From the bottom of my heart, I did not accept a marriage arranged by a matchmaker, so I packed my bags and moved from Long Lama to my second brother's farm in Miri.

After nine months of dating, we got engaged. Soon after, my

husband suggested that I move to his house. He thought that if we went abroad in the future, we would not be able to stay with my husband's family all the time, so he wanted to live in his house first to cultivate the relationship between mother-in-law and daughter-in-law. Because we were not married at the time, my family was unanimously opposed to it, but I decided to move in any way. My husband went abroad, but I stayed with my husband's family. In the morning, I helped my husband's family sell food, and in the afternoon, I went to learn tailoring by myself (1 pm-4 pm). I studied like this for about a year, which also meant living in my husband's house for 1 Year.

Until I was 21 years old, when I was leaving my hometown for Canada, my mother had been very sad for three months before she learned that I would leave Miri. She cried almost every day. I feel guilty for the parents who gave me birth and raised me. Although I look strong on the outside, I feel so sad inside. Only I know this feeling, and I can't explain it to others. It's so painful!

After a battle between heaven and man, for the sake of my future life, I spread my wings with guilty rationality and set foot on Canadian soil on March 17, 1973. My heart was full of excitement! I will always remember that day when I looked around and saw only green. People dressed in green clothes and wore clove decorations. There was a grand parade to celebrate St. Patrick's day. The streets were filled with floats, bands, and tens of thousands of spectators. It was lively. Extraordinary, that joyful scene is deeply imprinted in my memory. I finally came to Canada to reunite with my love, and then we registered our marriage at the local court on March 22 of the same year, and we finally got married!

"A beautiful acquaintance, with mutual affection and understanding."

"Our engagement photo."

"Our wedding photo."

"Our two daughters took a photo together in front of the third house we bought in Canada, with the address 8122."

Chapter 6
First Time Here, Remembering the Bitterness and Sweetness

I arrived in Canada on March 17, 1973. Even though it was spring, the weather was still cold. Life was like opening a brand new book for me, a book full of unfamiliar words and unknown plots. The feelings of loss, depression, hesitation, and homesickness I felt when I first arrived in a foreign country still linger in my mind.

I remember that at that time, I was faced with a strange environment, language barriers, and the impact of cultural differences. I was always enveloped by a sense of loneliness of "alone in a foreign land and a stranger." In this strange land, I gradually experienced the ups and downs of life.

In the 1970s, my love had the idea of immigrating. Since there was no Canadian Embassy in Malaysia at that time, he wrote directly to the Canadian Embassy in Hong Kong to inquire about the conditions for immigrating to Canada. After that, he applied for the job through the Canadian Embassy in Brunei. When immigrating, I successfully passed the specific entry policies and requirements set by the Canadian government, including age, work experience, educational background, language ability, etc., with full marks.

Canada in the 1970s appears to have been a period of relative economic stability and a relatively low cost of living. At that time, prices in Canada were very low, allowing many people to live a relatively comfortable life. I still remember that the prices of daily necessities at that time were quite affordable. 1 liter of milk only costs 0.25 Canadian dollars, a chicken only 1.5 yuan, and 1 gallon of gasoline only costs 4.5 yuan. Even the cost of sending a letter was very cheap. It only costs CAD 8 cents to send a letter from Canada to

Malaysia.

As for housing and transportation, an ordinary car only costs about 2,000 Canadian dollars, and a 1000-square-foot house only costs about 30,000 Canadian dollars. The price was affordable, which was a very attractive opportunity for new immigrants. Compared with domestic prices, these prices appeared quite reasonable, giving people hope for a future of possibilities. At that time, my husband's first job salary was Canadian dollars 4.2 per hour, which was not too low. It matched the price of goods and was enough to maintain a basic livelihood.

Overall, Canada at that time seemed to be a place with a relatively low cost of living and plenty of opportunities, attracting new immigrants looking for a better life. Prices, housing prices, and living costs were relatively low, providing people with more economic freedom and hope. It is for these reasons that my love decided to live in Canada permanently to make his future more secure.

I set foot on Canadian soil nearly a year later than my love. My husband did not find a suitable job in the first month after arriving in Canada. Everything was difficult at the beginning. The living conditions were not well-off at the beginning, so we had to rent a house. There is only a single bed in the room, but this little nest is full of our love and warmth.

Thank God, about 6 months after arriving in Canada, we received MYR 10,000 (approximately equivalent to CAD 4,000) from my love's family. This money became our down payment on our first home in 1973. When I was in the first house, my eldest daughter was born. I looked forward to getting better and better days and everything developing for the best.

Sure enough, we sold our first house in 1975 and made a profit of CAD 17,000. The proceeds helped us purchase a second property with a down payment of approximately CAD$20,000. This way, we can easily meet the monthly payments. The second house, the house number is 4331, my second daughter was born, and I longed for the days to become more and more prosperous.

During the period from 1973 to 1978, the family's livelihood mainly depended on love, and we lived a life of "men taking care of the outside and women taking care of the house." I also occasionally go to his landlady's place to help with housework and earn some extra living expenses.

We lived in the second house until 1979, when we moved to the third house we bought, with house number 8122, because there was a school nearby and it was convenient for our children to attend classes. When I was in the third house, my youngest son was born, and I firmly believed that life was getting better and better.

Until 1989, we spent money to build house number 228 and lived there for 20 years. In this house, my two daughters got married, and my son moved to another city to work.

My husband and I have also been involved in business and experienced setbacks where we lost all our money. But these experiences have taught us to be more cautious and also taught us more business wisdom. Gradually, we found the ropes of the business and learned more about how we operate.

I am a resilient person who strives to adapt to new environments, constantly strives to find my place, and does not want to feel helpless often. I started taking tailoring courses and later opened my tailoring shop, invested in real estate, and operated direct-selling products.

It is not easy to start a business. It is not easy for women to start a business. It is even more difficult to start a business in a foreign country. There is no background, no resources, and no support. The only support is yourself. During this period, I encountered countless hardships, experienced inner confusion, hesitation, and helplessness, and finally passed the most difficult period in starting a business.

I went to court four times in Canada and won each time. One of them was when an employee sued me for non-payment of wages. Another incident involved a tenant who, when I purchased a property, breached the contract and quietly moved out but left a cat in the house who made a mess and urinated and defecated. Seriously damaged the sanitary condition of the house. The tenant was eventually ordered to pay nearly one year's rent.

Looking back on the time from the ignorant teenagers and girls to the calm old married couple now, I have been confused, hesitant, and emotional. Fortunately, I have lived up to the past. I have been on the road of immigration for more than 50 years, and I have been filled with emotions and insights along the way.

Time flies, and now it has been rooted in this land for 50 years. This journey has been full of challenges but also full of growth and opportunity. Canada has become my second home in life, and I am proud to have built a family and career here. The most important thing I have learned is that no matter where I am, as long as I keep moving forward, face courage, and overcome adversity; a good life will be there waving at me.

"Newly arrived, I recall the bitter (hardships) and cherish the sweet moments."

"Over 50 years ago, when we first arrived in Canada, we were youthful and vibrant."

"The young us took photos in the snow and didn't feel cold at all."

1972 COST OF LIVING	
LIVING	
New House	$27,600.00
Average Income	$11,859.00 per year
New Car	$3,853.00
Average Rent	$165.00 per month
Tuition to Harvard University	$2,800.00 per year
Movie Ticket	$1.75 each
Gasoline	55¢ per gallon
United States Postage Stamp	8¢ each
FOOD	
Granulated Sugar	65¢ for 5 pounds
Vitamin D Milk	$1.20 per gallon
Ground Coffee	99¢ per pound
Bacon	83¢ per pound
Eggs	45¢ per dozen
Fresh Ground Hamburger	64¢ per pound
Fresh Baked Bread	25¢ per loaf
SeekPublishing	Remember When	1972

"The cost of living in Canada during the 1970s was relatively inexpensive."

"A middle-aged couple's photo."。

24

Chapter 7
Your Existence is My Future

No one can predict which will come first, tomorrow or the accident. The emptiness during the accident and the helplessness afterward are beyond our control. I recall that in 1977, on a Friday like any other day, I took my two daughters, the elder being 4 years old and the younger 4 months old, to pick up my love.

The only difference was the sudden car accident, adding another twist to my already uneven life.

After picking up my husband, as a family of four passed through an intersection, a car lost control and collided with the driver's seat, forming a V-shape impact with my car. Due to the force concentrated on the driver's seat, I tore my neck muscles, and then... I felt pain in the spinal nerves in my back, with a significant bump on my head from the collision. Fortunately, the occupants of the other car were generally unharmed.

The car accident has passed, but my nightmare has just begun. I sought medical help due to unexplained pain.

The aftermath of the car accident affected my sleep, leading to long-term insomnia, splitting headaches, and mental stress. At my weakest, even the ring of a phone would startle me, and I'd be in a bad mood if others spoke loudly.

In desperation, I visited a doctor at a private clinic. Perhaps I didn't encounter a good doctor. The doctor didn't inquire much but swiftly concluded that I had depression, prescribing medication for it. After six months of taking the medication, I found myself in the emergency department of a government hospital. Overdosing on the medication caused side effects such as indigestion and difficulty breathing, requiring additional antibiotics.

Upon returning to the same doctor, he prescribed a different medicine this time. The new medicine, placed under the tongue, quickly alleviated my rapid heartbeat. However, a few weeks later, I found myself back in the emergency department due to abnormal EKG results. Fortunately, before entering the emergency department for the second time, I brought all the medicines I had taken with me. The doctor there, upon reviewing my medications, suspected their unsuitability for my symptoms and feared for my life. The electrocardiogram was also found to be abnormal.

This time, they advised against seeing the doctor in that private clinic again and introduced me to another doctor. This marked a crucial turning point in my life. It was Dr. Brian Fernandes who became the first angel in my life, helping me quit all the dependency drugs I had been taking for three years (1978-1980). I always desired to have another child, but Dr. Fernandes informed me that continuing the medication would hinder that possibility. I had to stop the medication to have any hope of realizing my dream.

Dr. Brian Fernandes explained that the car accident had caused long-term insomnia and mental depression. Some symptoms resembled depression, but it wasn't depression. The previous medications were unsuitable for me, and the treatment I needed should focus more on physical therapy, massage, bone reshaping, and encouragement to engage in appropriate exercises. Thus, I started running, sometimes day and night, allowing me to sleep peacefully until dawn without relying on drugs.

Throughout the treatment, to distract from anxiety and pain, I maintained a full schedule. I worked part- time in the mall and took tailoring classes, striving to live a healthy and active life like a normal person to avoid overthinking. During work, I encountered my godmother, Mrs. Byrne Hindley. She became my second angel, caring for my well-being, offering encouragement, and showering me with love. Even when I called her at two or three in the morning, she patiently listened to my complaints. My relationship with my godmother endures to this day, making her a noble presence in my life. I am fortunate to have her accompany me through that challenging journey!

In those unforgettable years, to break free from the clutches of drug addiction, I actively collaborated with the doctor, adhering to every instruction. Many times, in pain, I wanted to give up, to scream, feeling the difficulty akin to taking drugs, unable to endure without relief.

Yet, I knew I was unwilling to fall at this juncture. With an unwavering will, I warned myself to "stand up" after overcoming it, to live, work, think, and communicate normally like ordinary people from sunrise to sunset each day. If you had interacted with me during that time, you might have thought me kind and humble, always wearing a smile and readily accommodating others' requests. You wouldn't know the immense effort I invested in living a normal life like you. Aside from my godmother, I refrained from discussing my illness with friends or even my children to alleviate their anxiety. I harbored a fear that others would regard me strangely and that I should feel ashamed. I believed I wasn't a normal person due to illness and drug addiction, even considering having a child a luxury.

I reminded myself that, having come this far, I couldn't give up now. I gritted my teeth, persisted, gradually reducing medication, reserving it for when absolutely necessary. In the final stage, the doctor declared me cured, granting the green light to have another child! At this juncture, I caution some patients that true healing may not result from consuming copious amounts of medication but from taking appropriate medication for genuine health.

Later, Dr. Brian Fernandes informed me that, in his over 40-year career, only five patients had successfully stopped taking that type of medication, and I was one of them. This doctor became my lifesaver, enabling me to have my son. Subsequently, whenever I fell ill, I sought his treatment. He claimed to be my family doctor for over 40 years, akin to family. I am profoundly grateful to him.

In the fourth year, 1981, at the age of 31, I successfully experienced a rebirth. Later, I successfully conceived my younger son, giving birth to a healthy child in November 1982. He was nine years younger than my eldest daughter. Witnessing the adorable face of my newborn son brought tears to my eyes. My resolute will empowered me to overcome the disease and drug addiction, fulfilling my dream!

Reflecting on those challenging and dark times, I actively maintained a semblance of normalcy, facing each day with fortitude. My primary belief, sustaining me to the end, was the desire to experience the joy of being a mother again. Looking back, I express gratitude to my younger self for enduring, not surrendering, molding the future me, and providing the unparalleled courage to navigate the excitement of the latter half of my life! I also extend gratitude to my son for being mine, affording me another chance at motherhood, enriching my life, and contributing to my becoming a better version of myself.

A saying goes, dreams are the most beautiful, yet living each day carefree is an almost impossible dream. For me, encountering the two angels in my life elucidated the concept of great love. They instilled in me the belief that society abounds with love, transforming my life into a beautiful dream. I anticipate meeting many angels who will bravely support my dreams. Simultaneously, I have become an angel for others, aspiring that everyone can not only harbor beautiful dreams but also transform into myriad angels, aiding others in realizing their dreams and making society a better place!

"Your presence, my future."

"I joyfully drive the first car I bought in Canada."

"At 21, I am full of dreams and expectations for the future."

Chapter 8
Hard Work, Fruitful Harvest

Having traversed the journey of cancer, undergone treatment, battled drug withdrawal, and emerged on the path to recovery, I found myself brimming with energy and set my sights on opening a tailor shop. In 1985, at the age of 33, I took the plunge and established my first tailor shop in downtown, christened (Canadiana) Tailor Shop.

During the inception of the store, my son was 2 and a half years old, my youngest daughter was 8, and my eldest daughter was 12. With three young children in need of careful attention and my husband working in another city, my weekdays involved juggling responsibilities at both home and the store. Commuting nearly half an hour from my original home to the store, I vividly recall waking up at 5 o'clock each morning to drive my daughters to school and my youngest son to daycare. Breakfast was often a mobile affair, consumed in the car before heading to the store. Realizing the strain of such a busy routine, I eventually decided to purchase a 3-bedroom apartment near the store. This move not only saved time but also facilitated an easier commute for my children to school.

In my youth, I pursued a one-year tailoring course at the "Rose Artificial Flower College" in my hometown, Miri, earning a diploma. Amidst cancer treatment from 1979 to 1980, I sought solace in self-improvement, working part-time and enrolling in an Italian tailoring class. I delved into five subjects, encompassing men's suits, trousers, shirts, women's clothing, and modifications. Though the period was challenging, it laid the groundwork for my future endeavors and fortified the foundation of my entrepreneurial journey. I expressed gratitude countless times for persevering through adversity, transforming my sewing passion into a career.

Tailoring is both my specialty and my hobby, and I am determined to master this intricate craft to achieve impeccable quality. My fervor for becoming a skilled tailor fueled my unwavering commitment.

From 1978 to 1985, especially during my part-time stint in a shopping mall, I frequently received requests from customers for alterations, repairs, and zipper replacements. I never turned down any request, recognizing that practice not only augmented family income but also honed my skills, understanding that proficiency is attained through dedicated practice.

Upon realizing my dream of opening the store, the business gradually gained momentum. Days became so hectic that I hardly found time to prepare meals. Resorting to restaurant deliveries on Mondays, Wednesdays, and Fridays, I dined out on Tuesdays, Thursdays, and Saturdays. Amidst this "war and chaos," I ensured a well-rounded education for my children, enrolling them in after-school programs, Chinese classes on Sundays, and music lessons in violin and piano to cultivate their temperament. This routine persisted until their college years, symbolizing my commitment to their holistic development.

In February 1989, tragedy struck when delivering lunch to my eldest daughter, then in junior high school. A slippery road caused an oncoming car to lose control, resulting in a head-on collision. The severe injuries forced me to convalesce at home. Despite occasional visits to the store, I handed over its management to employees due to mental health concerns.

After a year of recuperation, I resolved to make a comeback. Choosing the West Edmonton Mall, then the world's largest shopping mall, as the location for my new tailor shop, I named it West Edmonton Mall Tailors. Despite my absence, the business thrived, and I found myself swamped with orders upon my return. However, with escalating mall rents, I decided in 2006 to purchase two stores outside the mall, expanding and renovating the front to two floors and retaining the back as one floor, totaling approximately 3,000 square feet. The new store continued under the name West Edmonton Tailors, sans "Mall," signifying its independent location. As my children completed their college education in 2007, I opted to retire from school but maintained a strong rapport with customers. Some even sought tailoring services at my residence, but due to safety and privacy concerns, I deemed it inconvenient and declined.

During its zenith, my tailor shop boasted over ten tailors, with six working full-time and eight part-time, each contributing to our meticulous craftsmanship. The store specialized in high-end clothing, including custom-made men's and women's apparel, bridal gowns, suits, and coats. Customization services extended to sewing and modifying clothes. I personally undertook the creation of custom pieces within my capabilities, finding joy in fulfilling customers' dreams.

Measurement, fabric selection, line drawing, cutting, hemming, sewing, buttoning, ironing—the meticulous process of crafting customized garments echoed through the store. Masters under my guidance exhibited delicate and skillful hands, ensuring customer satisfaction with each stitch. The sewing machine's rhythmic "click, click, click" resonated throughout the store, signaling lively production. The meticulous processes became ingrained in my memory, defining an era where craftsmanship flourished.

As the business owner, my presence in the store was a daily occurrence. Customers entrusted their orders to me, finding solace in personal interactions. Business, however, is seldom smooth sailing, and jealousy was not absent from my entrepreneurial journey.

One part-time seamstress under my employ aspired to a full-time role despite her craftsmanship falling short. Adhering to Canadian laws, she worked part-time for 25 hours weekly, and her wages were never in arrears. A legal dispute arose when I failed to break down holiday pay and statutory holiday pay items on her payslip, combining the two payments into one. Though the court ultimately recognized all wages were paid, the lack of itemized detail on the payslip became a legal snag.

Thanks to positive word-of-mouth, the customer base expanded, establishing a commendable reputation for my shop. Customers flooded in, making my business increasingly popular. Even when unable to fulfill orders on time, I sought help from other tailor shops, emphasizing collaboration over competition.

Successfully transforming my tailor shop into a lucrative business, I achieved both personal satisfaction in pursuing tailoring and earned the recognition and respect of the community.

As a craftsman, I comprehended that each garment required unwavering dedication to infuse it with life. Seated before the sewing machine, my heart would find calmness, and I would immerse myself in the selfless act of creation. Customers once praised, "Bee, you can work on the water." Such affirmations and recognition alleviated the pressures of work, emphasizing the joy derived from pursuing a beloved craft. Doing what I loved and receiving acknowledgment for it felt like a genuine blessing.

To stay abreast of evolving trends and fashions, I perpetually embraced a learning mindset, observing more, learning more, and doing more. Fashion, I realized, follows cyclical patterns, with trends such as flared pants and high-waisted styles experiencing periodic resurgences. Iterating designs in harmony with current aesthetics birthed a spectrum of new beauties.

Among various types of customized clothing, my favorite remained crafting uniforms. A memorable instance involved a family seeking an identical police uniform for a little boy and his father. Personally tailoring the garments, the joyous moment of the boy and his father donning matching uniforms and capturing it in photographs nearly melted my heart.

Behind the tailoring of a bride's wedding dress lay the culmination of countless efforts, wisdom, inspiration, and art. The true enchantment of a wedding dress, however, lay in its ability to convey the bride's deepest emotions and wishes. Each bride aspired to have a unique wedding dress for life's most important moment—a garment that transcended mere clothing to symbolize the commencement of a beautiful dream.

Letters from brides post-wedding, expressing gratitude and including photos, brought immense joy. Witnessing a bride in a wedding dress meticulously designed and crafted by me, radiating her beauty and unique personality, filled me with pride. The intricate details and folds, every bead carefully placed, shimmered with extraordinary radiance, encapsulating the bride's innermost expectations. The satisfaction and happiness I brought to people within my capacity became a source of profound pride.

From 1985 to 2007, spanning 22 years, my tailor shop bore witness to industry fluctuations and shifts in fashion. Importantly, those who entered my store left with joy, either finding the perfect garment or wearing specially tailored clothes. Participating in significant occasions and creating cherished memories brought genuine happiness.

"Your presence, my future."

"I joyfully drive the first car I bought in Canada."

"At 21, I am full of dreams and expectations for the future."

"Hard work in entrepreneurship, fruitful rewards."

"Group photo of the 6th graduating class of Miri's 'Rose Artificial Flower Sewing Academy.'"

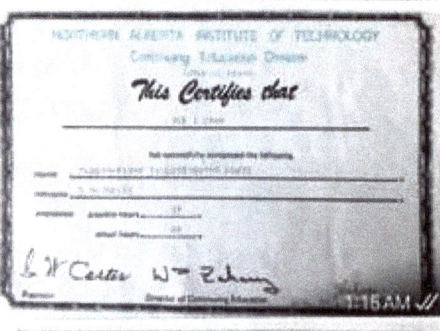

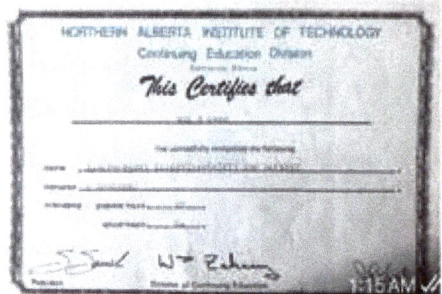

"I studied at the 'Rose Artificial Flower Sewing Academy' in Miri and obtained my graduation certificate."

"In the 1980s, I enrolled in an Italian tailoring course and obtained certificates in five subjects, including men's suits, men's trousers, men's shirts, women's clothing, and alterations."

"I worked at a store in the West Edmonton Mall, named West Edmonton Mall Tailors."

"A photo with the staff inside the store."

"I worked with my own hands, tirelessly rushing to complete the task."

"The customer left a message of thanks and sent a wedding photo."

"Taken beside the cash register inside the store."

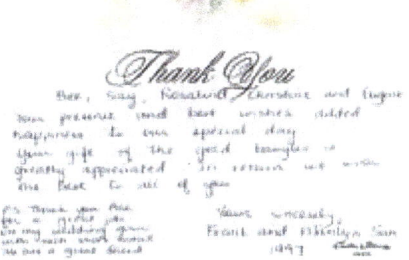

"Customer's thank-you note."

"A thank-you letter from a customer, expressing gratitude for tailoring her wedding dress and giving her a beautiful memory."

"The bride, wearing the wedding dress I personally tailored for her, displayed a joyful smile."

"The little boy wore the custom-made police uniform, identical to his father's, and the father and son happily posed for a photo together."

Thank You

James & Marie
Tambaoan

July 22, 2006

"The bride, extremely satisfied with my masterpiece, took a photo with me.

"After the wedding, the bride sent a thank-you card."

"My tailoring business has been recognized by customers, who often send photos wearing the finished products to share their joy."

Chapter 9
Build Your Own House. It's Your Home

The saying, "A house is the beginning of a home, and a home is the continuation of happiness," resonates deeply with me. In 1973, the first year my family arrived in Canada, we purchased our inaugural house in the quaint town of Whitecourt, Alberta. Two years later, in 1975, as I transitioned to work in the city of Edmonton, we sold our first home and acquired a second. This decision was influenced by the government's plan to build a school near the original location, a plan that, due to unforeseen factors, never materialized.

In 1979, we embraced another change, settling into our third home with the apt number 8122. Proximity to a school made this location particularly convenient for our children's education. Subsequently, as I embarked on my entrepreneurial journey, we purchased a three-bedroom apartment near the company. Eventually, our family relocated to the western province of Alberta, where we were fortunate to build our dream home.

The construction of our ideal house in 1989 marked a significant milestone. My husband and I personally selected the site, bought the land, chose materials, designed the plans, and assembled a construction team. Every detail received meticulous attention, demanding significant time and financial investment.

Throughout the construction process, I actively participated, from sketching plans to using wood and steel bars for the structure and even cultivating flowers in the garden with my own hands. The vibrant colors of the blossoms adorned the garden, enriching the canvas of our lives.

This house embodied all the criteria and aspirations for an ideal home. It boasted pleasing decor, spacious interiors, an ideal location, and a beautiful environment. Every day spent within its walls radiated sunshine and vitality for our family.

Beyond serving as a mere shelter, this dwelling became the habitat of my soul—a harbor woven with sweat and wisdom, a sanctuary for complete relaxation of body and mind, and a space for cultivating sentiments. In this unique haven, I discovered my peace and tranquility.

Fondly nicknamed "228's home," this house encapsulated many beautiful and unforgettable memories from the past 20 years. The echoes of children's laughter reverberating through the rooms as they played, the warmth of shared meals and celebrations with relatives and friends, and the leisurely moments tending to the garden—all formed a vivid tableau within these walls.

Featuring 2 living rooms, 2 kitchens, 7 rooms, 4 toilets, and a spacious garden, the house became our family's abode when my son was in the third grade. It offered stability, happiness, and a profound sense of belonging. We coexisted until our children flew the nest, marking the moment our two daughters married and our son established a family in another city. However, in 2009, my battle with stage three breast cancer left me physically depleted, and I faced the challenging decision to move out and settle in Vancouver.

Upon listing the house on the MLS (Multiple Listing Service) and placing it on the market, a lawyer couple with two children emerged as potential buyers. After a two-year search for a house in the area, they instantly fell in love with ours and placed a deposit on the same day. Given three months to vacate, the suddenness of it all stirred mixed emotions as I prepared to bid farewell to the home that had embraced my family for over two decades. The departure from my ideal home transcended physical relocation; it marked an emotional farewell. Year after year, time lingered within its walls, witnessing the growth of children, the aging of the couple, and the myriad stories that unfolded—intimate, happy, noisy, lively, quarrelsome, hurtful, silent, and lonely.

Upon leaving, the complexity of emotions overwhelmed me. Gazing at my house, where time had woven countless memories, a deep attachment took hold. Saying goodbye felt as poignant as parting from a beloved relative. While I longed to preserve the house, my health demanded otherwise. I had to entrust it to a new owner capable of caring for it. A new home could never replace the special place this ideal home held in my heart, yet I embraced this reality, for life presses forward.

Occasional visits to the house reassure me that the lawyer couple and their family continue to cherish and love it. Paradoxically, a tinge of inexplicable sadness accompanies this reassurance—I still find it challenging to let go.

Fortunate to have experienced such a home in my life, it stands as a testament to the ideals built with my own hands. This house, "228's home," holds a soul, encapsulating the stories and experiences that shaped my past. It allowed me to realize personal ideals, create beautiful memories, and served as a protective haven for my family. Even as I move forward, it will forever shine with warmth in my heart.

Build your own house, it's your home

"My ideal house is 228."。

"A corner of the garden in my ideal house 228, featuring a rockery and flowing water landscaping arrangement."

Chapter 10
Thousands of hardships make me stronger

In late 2006, a discovery changed the course of my life. A small, rice-like lump on my left breast triggered a sense of unease. The subsequent delay in seeking medical attention allowed the lump to progress into the third stage of breast cancer, growing to 11 centimeters. As my health deteriorated, a call from my younger brother and sister in Malaysia added complexity to my situation. My niece, the second daughter of my younger sister, expressed her desire to study in Canada and sought my support.

Despite my own health concerns, I made a pivotal decision in early 2007 to assist my niece in studying abroad. Concealing my illness, I navigated the complex process of securing a Canadian study visa for her. Financial challenges emerged, impacting my cash flow, but I pressed on, forcing a smile to conceal my anxiety, fear, and pain.

A year of relentless effort paid off in spring 2008 when my niece obtained her study visa. Urging her to leave for Canada swiftly, I wanted her to work part-time and contribute towards her education expenses. Concurrently, I faced my own health crisis. Upon her arrival in Canada, I drove her from the airport straight to handle numerous procedures, all while keeping my own physical condition concealed.

The reality of my breast cancer diagnosis struck during a routine health check. Neglected, the tumor had grown to an alarming size, reaching the third stage. The news was devastating for my family, but after the initial shock, they rallied behind me with unwavering support.

My husband took a two-month leave to accompany me through

the arduous journey of battling cancer. Surgery was initially planned, but the tumor's size necessitated preoperative chemotherapy. Despite the physical and emotional toll, I faced each day with determination. My son, who was offered job opportunities in two cities, chose to relocate to Calgary, respecting his decision despite my own selfish desires. Alone at home, I found strength in solitude, maintaining a balanced diet, a positive attitude, and emotional stability.

From May to December 2008, 12 rounds of chemotherapy tested my resilience. Following this, surgery in December successfully removed all cancer cells, and I proceeded to four months of recuperation.

Subsequent radiotherapy aimed to destroy any residual cancer cells. The physical and psychological challenges were immense, from weakness and hair loss to nausea and skin issues.

The journey from the diagnosis of stage 3 breast cancer to recovery spanned a year, from the summer of 2008 to the summer of 2009. It was a period marked by uncertainty, pain, and despair. Yet, with the unwavering support of my family and medical team, I emerged on the other side, fully recovering.

Reflecting on this dark period, I acknowledge the hesitancy and helplessness that pervaded my life. However, my love for myself and my family, coupled with the support of those around me, became the bedrock of my resilience. Through the darkest moments, it was this love that allowed me to navigate the challenges, overcome the disease, and embrace a future filled with light and hope.

Chapter 11
Vicissitudes of Life, Everlasting Friendship

The story of my enduring friendship with my boss and his husband, Ruth, and George McGillivray, spans from 1969 to the present, weaving through the unpredictable twists of fate.

In my youth, I had a passion for basketball and a close-knit team. Fate intervened when one of my teammates' sisters needed a replacement for her domestic help job. Although initially uncertain due to language barriers and self-doubt, I courageously accepted the job at the age of 17. This unique work experience began in the enchanting year of 1969.

My boss, employed by Shell in the Miri oil field, resided in Piasau Camp. The role involved caring for his husband's four young children, the youngest being just eight months old. The setting was idyllic— Piasau Camp, with its spacious wooden houses surrounded by casuarina trees, close to the sea, and seamlessly integrated with nature.

Despite initial worries, the job became more than a test of English skills; it evolved into an exercise of responsibility and compassion. My transition was made easier through guidance from my teammates, and I quickly adapted to the new role. The boss and his husband, easy-going and friendly, created a welcoming atmosphere, and I soon became the nanny for their children.

Daily interactions included the landlady teaching me recipes and cake-making from her Canadian homeland. This shared culinary experience became a moment of intimacy, and I quickly embraced the cooking techniques she imparted. The family's generosity extended to surprises brought from Canada during their vacations, often in the form of clothing gifts.

A small grievance lingered from the past. Years ago, a puppy of mine met an unfortunate fate under the boss's car, causing deep sorrow. Over 50 years later, upon hearing of my dog Lovely's passing, my boss expressed his regret, recalling the incident and acknowledging the pain it caused.

When I left the job in 1971, we expected our paths to diverge with time and distance. However, fate had different plans. I moved to Canada in 1973, coinciding with my boss's return due to an expired contract. Our communication increased, and the McGillivray family showered my newborn with thoughtful gifts.

Over 50 years later, our connection has grown beyond employer-employee ties; it has transformed into a lasting friendship. We exchange holiday cards, share meals, and celebrate together. Visiting my boss's home feels like connecting with old friends. In 2023, the couple celebrated their 60th wedding anniversary. Despite the passage of time, the warmth and kindness that welcomed me into their lives remain unchanged.

Reflecting on this journey, I realize that life's wonders often unfold unexpectedly. Embracing unforeseen opportunities can alter our trajectories and nurture enduring relationships. This experience not only facilitated my personal growth but also deepened my understanding of the enduring nature of true friendship. As time marches on, genuine friendships can withstand the test of years, remaining as unbreakable as they were in the past.

"Through the changes and hardships, the friendship remains steadfast."

"My spouse and I took a photo with the boss and his wife, Ruth & George McGillivray."

"I often visit the boss and his wife."

"When the boss and his wife's daughter, Donna McGillivray, got married, I was invited to attend the wedding."

"Having time to have dinner and chat with friends is one of the great pleasures in l̄

Chapter 12
You Are the Angel of My Life

In 1978, I encountered a life-altering moment when I crossed paths with my godmother, Mrs. Byrne Hindley. We worked together in a shopping mall, and during that time, I faced the aftermath of a serious car accident that left both my body and spirit deeply wounded. Coping with physical pain led me down a path of medication dependency, and the toll on my well-being was evident in my dull eyes and indifferent expression as if life had lost its meaning.

It was my godmother who saw through my struggle. Despite my initial instinct to deny the issue, trust gradually built between us, and I found the courage to share my predicament. What unfolded next warmed my heart—she didn't blame or judge me; instead, she extended her hand without hesitation. Like a mother, she cared for me, offering support and guidance. Her unwavering kindness became a beacon of light in the darkest chapter of my life, revealing the angelic presence that she embodied.

During nights when sleep eluded me, I would call her at 2 or 3 in the morning. She responded with patience, offering a listening ear, support, and valuable advice. Her willingness to travel from her home to be by my side showcased a selfless dedication that solidified the angelic image I held of her.

Her husband, Mr. David Hindley, a quiet businessman, expressed care in subtle yet profound ways. His gentle gestures, like holding and kissing the back of my hand, left a lasting impression. His passing at the age of 75 created a void and a sense of regret, but the memory of his tenderness remains etched in my heart.

The Hindley family, consisting of my godmother and her three children, became a second family to me. The bond we share is akin to that of brothers and sisters, fostering a warm and harmonious environment that brings happiness and satisfaction.

Over the course of 45 years, our relationship has deepened, and my godmother, now over 90 years old, faces the challenges that come with age. Despite the limitations in her movement, I make regular visits, bringing food and daily necessities, striving to care for her and ensure her comfort. She is not only a treasure to her family but a cherished presence in my heart. I wish her good health and a long life, for she appeared when I needed her most, encouraging me to face life with strength and a smile, ensuring a beautiful future lies ahead.

"You are the angel in my life."

"I am celebrating my godmother's birthday."

"A photo of me with my eldest daughter, godbrother David Hindley, and godsister Donna Lynn Hindley."

"My godmother, Bryne Hindley, is celebrating her 90th birthday."

Take a photo with your godmother and her family。

Chapter 13
Complement Each Other; The Best Partner

Celebrating our 50th golden wedding anniversary, my beloved Say Chan and I reflect on the incredible journey of the past half-century. Through ups and downs, we've weathered life's storms hand in hand, witnessing the most breathtaking views, navigating the highs and lows, composing the symphony of life with laughter and tears. What stands out the most is that we're still together.

Our personalities couldn't be more different—while I'm outgoing and lively, my partner is quiet and gentle. Yet, in the 50 years we've spent together, we've come to appreciate the beauty of our differences. Marriage requires management and mutual adjustment; it's not about being together because of similar personalities. The conflicts that arise in our lives become opportunities for our personalities to complement each other, leading to mutual happiness.

Our journey began in the 1970s when we left our hometowns in Miri and embarked on a hopeful journey to Canada for a better future. We faced the challenges of adapting to a new culture, language, and environment, but our resilience saw us through. Starting from scratch, we worked hard, persevered, and laid the foundation for our lives in a foreign country.

In those early years, while I cared for our children at home, my husband focused on his career as a technician in an oil field company, working far from home. We tolerated the distance for the sake of our family, understanding that our sacrifice was a crucial part of our shared journey.

As we both grew in our respective fields, our complementary traits became the driving force behind our success. My energetic and vivacious nature complemented my partner's calmness and wisdom, creating a synergy that honed our skills and quietly accumulated wealth. Together, we ventured into real estate and achieved significant profits.

Our success isn't just the result of individual efforts but stems from shared goals. My enthusiasm inspires my partner to be more positive, while his wisdom grounds me, making me more rational and mature.

Together, we've built a thriving business and established a place for ourselves in Canada.

Life, however, is not without challenges. Financial and psychological pressures loomed large, especially in the beginning. Yet, our tenacity and trust in each other helped us overcome every obstacle.

Disagreements were approached with emotional control, and we refrained from quarreling in front of our children. Instead, we actively resolved conflicts and sought peace.

Now, after 50 years in Canada, our business thrives, and we lead a comfortable life. Our family has grown, and the laughter of our grandchildren echoes through our home. While time has left its mark, our feelings remain as strong as ever.

To young couples, I would say that love isn't about finding someone exactly like you. It's about finding someone willing to grow with you and face life together. Regardless of personality differences, a common goal and unwavering belief can help a marriage withstand the test of time, shining with eternal light, just like ours.

As we celebrate our 50th golden wedding anniversary on March 22, 2023, we hope to share the joy with the world. Our series of celebration activities included inviting Liu Yun to be our anchor, ensuring that the entire world can join us in the festivities. The night was filled with songs expressing the depth of our feelings, including "Have I Told You Lately," "You Raise Me Up," and many more.

In our strong love, I hope our children and grandchildren find inspiration for their own happiness. May they understand that the enduring love between parents is not just a precious inheritance but also the most valuable education imparted to them.

"Complementing each other, the best partners."

"Traveling and taking photos, making every moment of life count."

"The two of us, who love traveling, often take photos during our journeys."。

"On March 22, 2023, we celebrated our 50th golden wedding anniversary, and our son joined us for a meal to celebrate."

"Being with my beloved, I feel indescribable happiness."

"During the trip, I tried kayaking."

"My partner and I enjoy traveling and exploring nature. The photo was taken during our visit to the Gold Coast in Queensland, Australia, when the 2018 Commonwealth Games (XXI Commonwealth Games) were held there."

Chapter 14
Thank You Letter to My Love

My Dearest Love,

As I pen down these words, my heart swells with emotion, and a cascade of memories from the past 50 years unfolds before me like a cherished movie. Each frame is a precious moment, a blossom in the garden of our shared love.

We have weathered the storms and celebrated the joys, holding hands through 50 years of life's journey. Having you by my side has been the greatest blessing of my life. In 1973, we embarked on this adventure of marriage in Canada, a foreign land at the time. In our youth, brimming with energy and dreams, little did we imagine the decades of laughter, tears, and love that lay ahead.

Together, we faced challenges, forged ahead, and built a comfortable home in a foreign land. Our strength and bravery stemmed from knowing that you were my unwavering support, and I am, your motivation to persevere.

Love, we've learned, is a responsibility and an everlasting commitment. Despite differing dreams and values, amidst arguments and complaints, our love has kept us close and supported us through thick and thin.

You, my love, are the linchpin of my life. Your support, tolerance, and love envelop me in a cocoon of safety and joy. You are a diligent, honest, and reliable husband who tirelessly works for the happiness of our family. Even when work takes you away, I feel your enduring love. This, my dear, is the most precious gift of my life.

You've always encouraged me to chase my dreams. Owning a tailor shop has been my lifelong dream, and your silent support has empowered me to realize it. Your trust and understanding have fortified our marriage, and for that, I am eternally grateful.

Our pride and joy lie in the success and happiness of our three sons and daughters. We set an example for them, teaching the essence of true family and love. Their accomplishments are a testament to our enduring union. How fortunate I am that our love stands as a steadfast beacon, illuminating not only our path but also those of our children and grandchildren.

My love, over 50 years, we've faced challenges and relished beautiful moments. I want you to know that I love you more than words can express and appreciate your continued care and tolerance. May the coming years see us standing tall, blooming like flowers, sharing every moment, and crafting more beautiful memories together until our last breath.

A good partner makes life's journey a tapestry of shared joy. The warmth of having you is immeasurable.

As I conclude, allow me to dedicate a song to you, Su Rui's "Dedication":

Dedicate the long road to the distance Roses dedicated to love

What can I dedicate to you? My sweetheart

White clouds dedicated to the pasture Rivers contribute to the ocean

What can I dedicate to you?

My friend

What can I dedicate to you? I kept asking

I keep looking Keep thinking

White doves dedicated to the blue sky Starlight dedicated to the long night What can I dedicate to you?

My child

Dedicated to the earth during the rainy season Years dedicated to seasons

What can I dedicate to you? My parents

What can I dedicate to you? I kept asking

I keep looking Keep thinking

Forever loving you, Your Wife

Chapter 15
Love Replies with Deep Affection

My Dearest Wife,

Your letter is a burst of radiant fireworks, igniting a spectacle of memories in my heart that span 50 beautiful years. As I read your words, it feels like my thoughts are traversing through time, and every moment we've shared is a precious diamond, glittering in the river of our love.

We met, fell in love, and hand in hand, we've journeyed through half a century. In that era of longing, we set forth on a daring adventure to Canada, leaving our homes behind. The unknowns and challenges were plentiful, but with you beside me, that adventure was filled with hope, and the uncertainties were met with courage. Young and determined, we faced the unknown winds and rains, holding each other's hands tightly as we traversed the years together.

Our marriage didn't commence with grandeur; it quietly unfolded in peace and tranquility. Yet, this journey has painted a vibrant picture of life—full of sweetness, hardships, laughter, tears, and, most importantly, deep love.

In the tapestry of our life together, we've had our share of quarrels and complaints. Yet, each conflict has been a stepping stone, helping us understand each other better and fostering a deeper appreciation for what we have. Imperfections are a part of being human, but our love is perfect because it is true, committed, and persistent.

You've always been my pillar of strength, the most precious person in my life. Your tenacity, honesty, thriftiness, and reliability serve as beacons in my heart. Your selfless dedication to our family, especially during my times away from work, embodies the warmth of love. It is the most precious gift, and your trust and understanding have fortified our marriage.

You are the linchpin of my life, the driving force behind my every step. Your persistence, diligence, and sense of responsibility for our family have illuminated the true meaning of family and love. Your trust and tolerance form the bedrock of our marriage, without which, I would be incomplete.

Your dreams are my dreams, your wishes my wishes. If you wish to open a tailor shop, know that my unwavering support is behind you, for I recognize it as your dream, your talent, and your passion.

Witnessing you chase your dreams and realizing your ideals fills me with pride and happiness, for your success is our shared glory.

Our children are our pride, shining examples of our shared achievements and happiness. Their success and joy stand as a testament to our marriage and a source of collective pride.

In this seemingly long yet fleeting journey of marriage, we've faced countless challenges and shared numerous beautiful moments. Whether laughter or tears, I want you to know that I love you deeply and beyond measure. Our love is firm, real, and it is my pride—the greatest happiness of my life.

As the years unfold before us, let us continue to hold hands, moving forward together and creating more beautiful memories. Regardless of what life brings, our love remains loyal and eternal. Like a dazzling diamond, it radiates with colorful light, and our lives shine with brilliant luminosity.

You are the warmest sunshine in my life and the wellspring of my happiness. I love you, dear wife, forever.

Forever Yours,
Say Chan

Chapter 16
Be Well, My Children

My Dearest Children,

As I write this letter, my heart swells with pride and overwhelming love for each of you. You are the most precious gifts in my life, my cherished babies, and nothing in this world is more important to me than your well-being and happiness.

Rosaline, Christine, and Eugene, you are my pride and joy. No matter how successful my career may be, raising you into independent and strong adults has been my greatest achievement. From the early days, I instilled in you the values of autonomy, responsibility, and the importance of pursuing your dreams. I encouraged you to think independently, solve problems on your own, and believe that you could achieve anything you set your mind to.

Balancing work and family was not always easy, but you were my priority. I picked you up from school, took you to doctor appointments, and ensured your daily needs were met. Invisibly, your interactions with customers in the store developed your social skills, preparing you to navigate the world with ease. I may have had moments of guilt for not doing better, but seeing you grow into grateful, filial, healthy, and safe individuals makes me the happiest person.

The mutual understanding and tolerance between us have been crucial as you grew into adults with different personalities and life choices. Our ability to understand, agree, tolerate, and compromise has been the foundation of our harmonious family relationship.

Music has become an integral part of our lives, a gift that transcends language and cultivates character. Learning the piano and violin was not just about creating musicians but instilling perseverance and the ability to overcome difficulties. I watched as the harsh sounds of the early days turned into harmonious melodies, reflecting your growth and teaching you to find beauty in life's challenges.

Rosaline, your journey into music, from learning the violin to performing on international stages, filled me with immense pride. Although your university studies took a different path, your success in the field of accounting showcases your adaptability and determination.

Christine, your love for learning and your role as a high school English teacher bring me great joy. Your dedication to education and the impact you have on your students make me proud beyond words.

Eugene, your birth marked a turning point in my life, and watching you grow into a successful individual in computer engineering, and building your own family, fills me with pride and gratitude.

As you all have your own families and careers, you may not become master musicians, but the joy and value you find in the world of musical notes is a testament to the perseverance and love we've shared. Music will forever be a lifelong treasure, a catharsis of emotions, and a source of inspiration for each of you to play your own melody on the stage of life.

My dream is for the love I have for you to be a never-ending movement, passing on warmth and hope to the next generation. You are the eternal notes in the beautiful symphony of our family.

With all my love,
Your mother

"Be well, my children."

"The young me with a toddler in a photo." "The young us with a family portrait of our children."

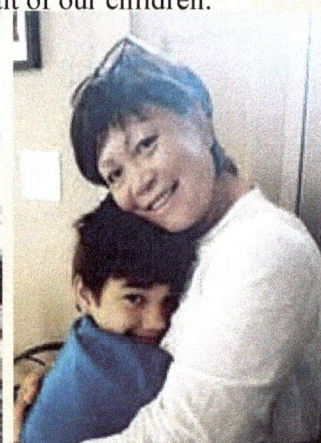

Daily photos with family。

"When my young daughter was a child, I was holding her during a summer carnival, as captured in this photo."

"Kiss my darling."

"A photo of my children, from left to right: my youngest daughter Christine, my youngest son Eugene, and my eldest daughter Rosaline."

"A happy family portrait of five."

Look back and smile

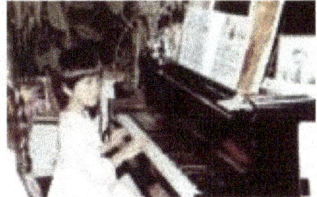

A photo of my young daughter from her childhood."

"A photo of my young son from his childhood."

"My young daughter is practicing the piano."

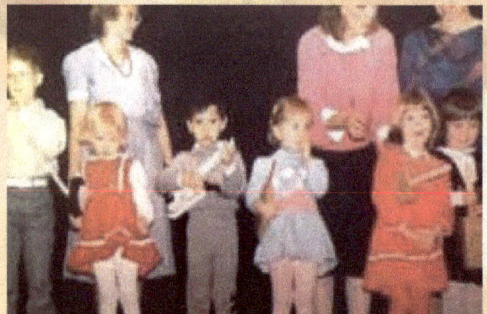

"When my young son was a child, he often performed on stage with the violin."。

"A photo taken during my son's family trip."

"A photo of my partner and me with our youngest son's family."

66

"Having a meal with my eldest daughter's family."

"Enjoying the mountains and waters with my family, what a joy!"

"Witnessing my child grow up and build a family and career."

"A photo with my young child."

"For my youngest son Junguang's 5th birthday, the whole family gathered together to celebrate."

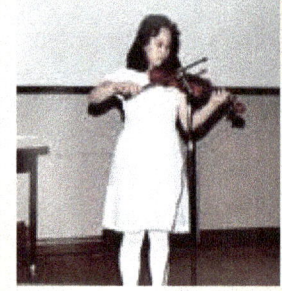

"A photo of me holding my 3-year-old eldest daughter."

"A photo of my eldest daughter when she participated in a violin competition as a child."

"A photo with my youngest daughter and son at my eldest daughter's college graduation."

"Enjoying family happiness with my descendants!"

Chapter 17
Letter to My Dear Son

My Dearest Son Eugene,

As I pen down these words, my heart is filled with an abundance of love and gratitude for the remarkable journey we've shared. You are the most precious gift in my life, and I want you to know the incredible story of your origins, a story of resilience, dedication, and the unbreakable bond between a mother and her child.

In 1977, life presented me with a tremendous challenge. A severe car accident left me grappling with physical and mental pain. The prescribed medication, meant to heal, unintentionally led me down a path of dependency. In those difficult times, I faced a choice – to succumb to despair or to rise above it for the possibility of experiencing the joy of motherhood once again.

With you as my motivation, I embarked on a challenging journey of recovery, overcoming addiction, and regaining my health. Your birth in 1982 was a moment of pure joy and emotion beyond words. You, my dear son, are the miracle that gave me the strength to start anew. From that moment, I made a solemn vow to give you the best life possible, no matter the obstacles that lay ahead.

The establishment of my own business in 1985 brought a new set of challenges. The demands of entrepreneurship led to the decision to enroll you in daycare at a tender age. While reluctant and burdened by guilt, I recognized that it was a decision made out of love and the pursuit of providing you with the care you deserved. From kindergarten to college, you stood by my side, helping in the store and sharing in the journey of life.

Throughout your upbringing, I endeavored to nurture you with care and dedication. Encouraging your study of music wasn't just about appreciating art; it was a deliberate choice to cultivate your patience, discipline, and creativity. Simultaneously, I emphasized the importance of academic knowledge, recognizing it as a powerful tool to build a solid foundation for your future.

Our journey has been marked by numerous difficulties and setbacks, but I never wavered in my commitment to you. Witnessing your growth, the start of your family, and your success in society fills me with immense pride and satisfaction. Your perseverance and talent assure me that your future is destined for endless possibilities, with the achievements you've earned being just the first steps on your path to success.

Son, always remember that you have a mother who silently sacrificed everything for you. My love and devotion are selfless, for you are the most precious treasure in my life. Whatever challenges you face in the future, believe that you have unwavering support, encouragement, and unconditional love from your mother.

As you continue to move forward on the road ahead, chasing your dreams and realizing your aspirations, carry with you the reminder of my everlasting love. I love you deeply, you are my pride, and you are the greatest achievement in my life.

Love you forever,

Your Mother

"A letter to my dear son."

"A family photo with my young child."

"A letter to my dear youngest daughter."

"A family photo with my youngest daughter."

"A letter to my dear eldest daughter."

Chapter 18
Letter to My Dear Younger Daughter

My Dearest Christine,

As I pour my heart into this letter, waves of emotion flood my soul. Time has gracefully woven a beautiful tapestry upon you, and witnessing your joyous family and successful career fills me with an inexplicable sense of relief. I am compelled to express the depth of my love for you and to convey my gratitude to God for the incredible gift of having you as my caring daughter.

From the moment you entered this world, your cries heralded the arrival of the most precious gift in my life. In those early months, you had a delicate life that required all my love and care. Yet, life's twists and turns, particularly the devastating car accident, tested me in ways I never imagined. My weakened body and spirit left me unable to care for you as I wished, and I carry a lasting sense of guilt for that difficult time. My child, I wronged you then, but you emerged as my sturdy pillar, displaying independence, a love for learning, and a strength that runs deep within your heart.

Your dedication to learning and your independent spirit have always been your defining traits. I recall your early passion for music, and I endeavored to support your dreams, recognizing your boundless potential. Your journey through college, choosing the path of Education, and eventually becoming an outstanding high school English teacher make me incredibly proud. Your professionalism, passion for education, and the positive impact you have on your students deeply impress me.

Your true dowry isn't measured in gold or silver wealth; rather, it is the gift of education and boundless love that I have bestowed upon you. Witnessing you leverage these gifts to not only achieve success but also radiate happiness within your own family fills my heart with immense pride. Balancing family and career with such grace is a testament to your strength.

I've always acknowledged that your success stems from your hard work and perseverance, yet I want you to know that, behind the scenes, I have silently stood as your unwavering support.

My dear daughter, no matter how successful you become or how joyous your family life may be, always remember that I am your steadfast support, and my love for you knows no bounds. Regardless of what the future holds, you carry the enduring love and support of a mother, and you will never be alone.

Continue to be true to yourself, pursue your dreams, and care for your family. Know that I am always by your side, enveloping you with my deep love and blessings.

Love you forever,

Your Mother

"A letter to my dear son."

"A family photo with my young child."

"A letter to my dear youngest daughter."

"A family photo with my youngest daughter."

"A letter to my dear eldest daughter."

Chapter 19
Letter to My Dear Elder Daughter

My Dearest Rosaline,

I hope these words find their way to the depths of your heart, carrying the love and pride that I hold for you, a love that remains unwavering no matter what challenges life may throw your way. You are my caring little cotton-padded jacket, a source of warmth and strength that has been a constant in my life.

I vividly recall the year our family embarked on a new life in Canada, and you entered this world like a radiant star, adorning our family with joy. Those early days were not without their struggles, and as a first-time mother, I navigated the challenges with little experience and often in haste. Yet, your presence was a comforting anchor in this foreign land, my only familial tie. With you by my side, the initial loneliness and disorientation of being a stranger in a new place began to fade, and I discovered my rhythm in this unfamiliar environment. It was you, my dear, who gave me the strength and motivation to move forward.

An incident from your infancy still echoes in my memory. At eight months old, while our house was being repainted, a momentary lapse led to a fall from the crib. The subsequent months were marked by hospital visits, high fevers, and worry. Your strength and resilience during that challenging time were a testament to the remarkable spirit you possess. The fear and heartbreak I experienced during that period have lingered, a reminder of your early battles and triumphs.

From a young age, you displayed remarkable strength and intelligence. At the tender age of 12, you were already assisting me in the complexities of my business. Your ingenuity and problem-solving skills were evident, not only in business matters but also in your caring nature towards your younger siblings. You became an exceptional sister, bringing warmth, care, and laughter to our lives. During my battle with breast cancer, your companionship was a shining light, dispelling the darkness and instilling a sense of safety and strength.

I have dedicated myself to providing you with the best opportunities to pursue your dreams. I remember the days when you immersed yourself in the study of music, your passion evident in every practice session. Your talent and perseverance were undeniable, and I firmly believe that your future holds brilliance.

I spared no effort in ensuring you received the best education and had the opportunity to attend a prestigious university. I have always held the belief that education is the key to changing one's destiny, and you have proven this truth with your hard-earned successes in your career. Your achievements fill me with pride, knowing that each milestone is a testament to your dedication.

Most importantly, you have found love, married a wonderful man, and embarked on the beautiful journey of creating your own family. Witnessing your happiness and observing the love you pour into your own role as a mother brings me immeasurable joy. May your family always be blessed with boundless joy and happiness.

My precious daughter, I want you to know that I will forever be by your side—supporting you, loving you, and offering prayers for your well-being. You are my baby, my pride, my everything. May your daily life be filled with an abundance of love and warmth.

Deeply in love with you,

Your Mother

"A letter to my dear son."

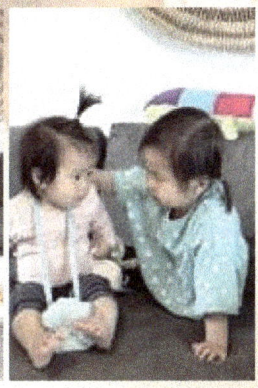

"A family photo with my young child."

"A letter to my dear youngest daughter."

"A family photo with my youngest daughter."

"A letter to my dear eldest daughter."

Chapter 20
A Letter to Dear Jun Yi

My Dearest Jun Yi,

As I sit down to pen this letter, my heart is brimming with gratitude and joy, sentiments that words may not fully capture, but I feel compelled to express nonetheless. Your arrival in my life, especially at this stage in my seventies, has brought me immense relief and happiness, filling the void that lingered in the realm of music. I may not convey the depth of my emotions adequately, but I wish to attempt to express my thanks through these words.

As my three children gradually moved away from the enchanting world of music, I harbored a sense of regret and disappointment. Music, you see, has always been my profound love, an integral part of my existence. So, when I encountered you, more than two decades ago, stepping into the music scene, coinciding with the period my children were relinquishing their musical pursuits, it felt like fate had woven our paths together. Our deeper communication on the platform, especially through your active Facebook fan group, intensified our connection.

Dear Jun Yi, I want to convey a heartfelt "Thank you." The interaction we've shared on this platform has brought joy and cheer into my life. Your encouragement has been a beacon, inspiring me to open my heart and return to Malaysia to celebrate my 70th birthday with family and relatives and, later, my 71st birthday with a group of basketball sisters.

Your presence, marking the beginning of our bond as an adopted son, transformed everything. It was as if a beam of radiant sunlight pierced through dark clouds, casting a splendid golden hue and infusing my world with boundless warmth and hope. Your musical prowess and unwavering dedication have deeply moved me. Your singing and performances are enchanting, transporting me back to the vibrant and energetic years of my youth.

Beyond your artistic talents, you embody kindness and compassion. Our shared experiences resonate, and your solace and care became a healing balm during the unbearable pain of losing my beloved furry friend. Through your live broadcasts, I witnessed your genuine love for music, and your companionship and support bring me immense happiness and contentment.

Always remember, you are not just my adopted son; you are a radiant star illuminating my life. Continue to tread the path of music with courage and determination, persisting in the pursuit of your dreams. Your music is not merely an art form; it is a force capable of touching hearts and changing the world.

Your presence has added hues of color to my life, making it rich with hopes and dreams. May your musical journey be smooth, and may our relationship remain close and warm throughout. Thank you for being a part of my life, my dear kid.

Forever loving you,

Mother.

"A letter to my dear Junyi."

"A group photo with Junyi's fan club and music friends."

I'm so happy to have met you

"On November 8, 2022, accompanied by my eldest daughter and granddaughter, I met Teacher Shen Huaxing (TONY SIM, left) and Junyi (second from the left) for the first time, and we were at Ji.""A group photo at the hotel in Kuala Lumpur. A photo with Teacher Shen Huaxing (TONY SIM) and Junyi."

Chapter 21
I'm So Happy to Have Met You

As I take a moment to reflect on the incredible journey of this friendship, my heart overflows with joy and gratitude. The twists and turns of fate have brought us together in a way that feels almost magical.

In my seventies, I never anticipated that I would be blessed with the friendship of someone as remarkable as Jun Yi, a Malaysian artist, who, despite the significant age difference, has become a cherished friend. Life has a way of surprising us with its wonders.

Our connection began when I joined the "Zhang Shuirong Family" fan group, introduced by my beloved. Initially indifferent to bloggers and anchors, I stumbled upon Juin Yi during a live broadcast with Zhang Shuirong. The camaraderie and harmony he shared with fellow singers captivated me. It prompted me to reach out to him for assistance in procuring albums, thus initiating our interaction.

From being a silent observer in his live broadcasts, I gained the confidence to leave messages, expressing my admiration. During the late stages of the COVID-19 pandemic, he transitioned to singing live, attracting new foreign fans, myself included. Eventually, I officially joined his fan club and singer group on Facebook in April 2022.

Our friendship evolved through messages, phone calls, and the endearing term "Mommy" that Jun Yi affectionately bestowed upon me. Despite the geographical distance between Canada and West Malaysia, our communication remained seamless. I became not just a fan but a caring motherly figure, concerned about his well-being and daily life.

The revelation of Jun Yi's birth year, 1979, struck a chord deep within me. It brought healing to a long-standing desire for another child, a dream that had lingered for over 40 years. Meeting him in person for the first time in Kuala Lumpur on November 8, 2022, accompanied by my eldest daughter and granddaughter, was an emotional and delightful experience. Subsequent meetings in Singapore and Kuala Lumpur reinforced the warmth of our bond.

An unexpected connection emerged when I discovered that Jun Yi was a classmate and good friend of my niece-in-law's brother, sharing the same hometown and serving as her son's music teacher. The serendipity of these discoveries magnified the beauty of our intertwined destinies.

There are countless anecdotes and coincidences, like the matching license plate numbers and similar childhood experiences, which only deepened our connection. In our two years of friendship, I've shared my life experiences, provided guidance, and watched Jun Yi grow into a successful online personality and artist.

In my posts to the fan club and singer group, I've expressed the sentiment that meeting Jun Yi is a testament to the beauty of life. Cherishing every moment, celebrating ordinary days, and valuing the people around us are the true treasures of life. As a motherly figure, I extend my wishes for his success, good health, and a life free from hardships.

The bond we share is beyond that of ordinary friends; it resembles a mother-son relationship, a rare and precious connection that I hold dear.

"A letter to my dear Junyi."

"A group photo with Junyi's fan club and music friends."

I'm so happy to have met you

"On November 8, 2022, accompanied by my eldest daughter and granddaughter, I met Teacher Shen Huaxing (TONY SIM, left) and Junyi (second from the left) for the first time, and we were at Ji.""A group photo at the hotel in Kuala Lumpur. A photo with Teacher Shen Huaxing (TONY SIM) and Junyi."

"The third meeting was on December 14th in Kuala Lumpur, where we gathered with fans from various places to celebrate Junyi's birthday. I remember the atmosphere at the event was lively and warm."

"The second time I met Junyi was on December 10, 2022, when I attended Junyi's fan meeting with fans in Singapore."

Chapter 22
Canada During the Epidemic

In 2020, an unprecedented pandemic broke out worldwide—COVID-19, which originated in Wuhan, China, and spread globally, bringing the world to a standstill. The threat of COVID-19 induced panic as the number of cases surged, enveloping society in extreme anxiety and insecurity. Following the outbreak in Canada, Canadian provinces successively declared a state of emergency starting in mid-March. This led to the suspension of "non-essential" business activities and services, with people required to stay at home.

During this time, I had lived in Edmonton, Canada, for nearly 50 years, relishing the tranquility and prosperity of this beautiful city. However, the year brought a profound sense of unease and uncertainty for me and millions of Canadian families. As a travel enthusiast, I had planned exciting adventures throughout the year to explore different cultures, taste various cuisines, and create precious memories.

Yet, the sudden epidemic in the spring of 2020 compelled me to completely alter my lifestyle. The government issued stay-at-home orders, flights were canceled, and travel became impossible. The world, which once held unlimited possibilities, suddenly seemed small and perilous. The "home confinement order" not only restricted personal space but also affected the freedom the heart yearned for—a "confinement of the heart." Faced with the epidemic, compromises became inevitable.

People, faced with the spread of the epidemic, resembled frightened birds. Supermarket shelves emptied as people rushed to buy masks, disinfectant, toilet paper, and other daily necessities. Hospital beds quickly filled with confirmed patients, and medical staff worked tirelessly. Witnessing the increasing number of cases every day, my family and I felt anxious, worrying about ourselves and our loved ones. In the later stages of the epidemic, my husband and I also contracted the virus but fortunately recovered quickly.

The Canadian government swiftly implemented a series of emergency measures at the early stage of the epidemic, including blockades and travel restrictions, to control its spread. While these measures helped slow the epidemic, they also profoundly impacted the economy. The unemployment rate surged, causing many people to lose their jobs, and the family economy took a severe hit. Seeing many people around me facing financial stress made me appreciate my stable life even more.

Adapting to the new normal became inevitable. During the days of isolation at home, I learned to adapt to a new lifestyle. Personally accustomed to traveling freely, I now needed to stay away from crowds, adhere to social distance regulations, wear a mask, and wash my hands frequently to ensure safety. This change might be more challenging for people of my age, but I understood its necessity.

Remote working became the new normal, online shopping replaced traditional methods, and video calls became the primary way to stay in touch with family and friends. Despite being a long-time supporter of technology, this year, I delved deeper into understanding and applying digital technology. I began using the Internet more to maintain social connections, stay in touch with family and friends, and share emotions and experiences. Losing the freedom of my body and mind turned out to be a blessing in disguise. However, staying at home more often also allowed my husband and me to spend more time with our children and grandchildren, bringing our hearts closer.

Amid this difficult moment, there were unexpected opportunities and turning points. A particularly special experience was becoming a fan of Jun Yi, a popular and powerful singer. His music, full of energy and sunshine, brought happiness and warmth during the epidemic through his live broadcasts. I grew to appreciate not only his musicianship but also his positive energy and interaction with the audience.

Gradually, I found myself liking him not just for his music but also for his personality. His optimism and love for life inspired me to face my life more positively. Actively joining his fan group connected me with like-minded individuals, leading to a deeper understanding of my idols and the discovery of real friends.

Every day, I couldn't wait to log in to the fan club and singer group to see everyone's posts and shares. This interaction made me feel warm as if I had a group of friends accompanying me on my journey. During this difficult time, we became a close-knit community by sharing joy and supporting each other.

As I often wrote posts, I developed a desire to write an autobiography. While this is a story for another time, these opportunities eventually led to the publication of my autobiography. Additionally, I regained my enjoyment of cooking and reading. With plenty of time, I immersed myself in the kitchen, paying more attention to ingredients and cooking methods, focusing on knife skills, stirring, and cooking processes. This concentration brought satisfaction, reducing stress in daily life and making me feel calmer and more relaxed. It was like opening a good book and quickly immersing myself in a whole new world. Reading novels, poetry, or art books inspired my own creative work and new ideas.

In modern fast-paced life, returning to simple and beautiful things like cooking and reading became essential for finding inner satisfaction. By rediscovering these joys, I achieved better life balance, increased happiness, and lived a richer life. Looking back after the epidemic, during the lockdown period, life slowed down, almost stopping, providing an opportunity to appreciate the scenery of life. Sometimes, the pace of life is too fast, causing us to overlook its beauty. Life can be simple. Stop for a moment and look back, enjoying and reminiscing about the beauty of spending time at home. It also made me more grateful for every moment in life that explodes like fireworks.

The epidemic changed everything, but behind all these changes, I also witnessed the resilience and unity of the Canadian people. Volunteers from community organizations helped those in need, medical workers heroically worked on the front lines, and the government took measures such as emergency wage subsidies, recovery subsidies, and emergency rent subsidies to support affected businesses, organizations, and individuals while ensuring the stable operation of the medical system.

Chapter 23
Celebrating 70th Birthday, Full of Happiness

Having resided in Canada for nearly 50 years, I make a point to return to my hometown to reconnect with family and friends almost every year. Boarding the flight back to my hometown in November 2022, I feel a heightened sense of anticipation. I am well aware that this particular trip will be an unforgettable journey, as my hometown, Miri, is about to set the stage for my 70th birthday celebration. This promises to be a special and momentous day, and my heart is brimming with boundless excitement and emotion.

Unfortunately, due to the expiration of my husband's medical insurance, she couldn't accompany me on the journey. It took about three weeks before she could join me in Miri.

Finally, the much-anticipated day of my birthday celebration, November 12, 2022, arrived. The celebration took place at the "Shiweitian Seafood Restaurant," where 15 tables were set up for the occasion. My eldest daughter, granddaughter, and I arrived early. Upon entering the restaurant, we were taken aback by the vibrant decorations—gold and red adorned the venue, creating a festive atmosphere. The stage backdrop in the middle was adorned with colorful balloons and ribbons, featuring golden English balloons spelling out "HAPPY BIRTHDAY" alongside a three-layer cake on a small round table, making it incredibly eye-catching. Clad in a golden lace cheongsam, I suddenly felt a slight nervousness. I felt like a deer caught in the headlights, realizing I was the protagonist today, yet somehow not entirely ready. My primary motive was simply to gather with relatives and friends I seldom see, under the pretext of celebrating my birthday. The motive was as single and pure as that.

Relatives and friends gradually arrived, and as an elder, I distributed red envelopes to the unmarried juniors and children, offering wishes for their peace and happiness. As everyone gathered, whether by appointment or chance, I couldn't help but notice that many were dressed in red to celebrate my birthday. The venue was bathed in bright red, enhancing the joyfulness and liveliness of the occasion.

At the beginning of the banquet, delectable dishes were served one after another. People sat together, engaging in free-flowing conversations and laughter. Some relatives and friends had traveled from Brunei, West Malaysia, and Sarawak to attend the celebration. At that moment, my heart swelled with emotion and gratitude. Surrounded by people who love me and whom I love, I felt privileged to share this wonderful time.

One of the highlights was the presence of six friends from the girls' basketball team. We had grown up together in this small town, sharing countless moments of happiness. Reuniting felt like stepping back into our youthful days, reminiscing about carefree times, and laughing about our dreams and wishes. On this special day, I celebrated not only my birthday but also a long-lasting friendship.

The celebration reached its climax when, as the birthday celebrant, I was invited to the stage, witnessed by my six good sisters. The spotlight in my heart appeared once more, accompanied by the fluttering of the little deer within me. Feeling a mixture of anxiety and excitement, I slowly made my way to the stage. Listening to the blessings from everyone, we cut the cake together and sang "Ping Ju":

Never mind how it will end later, At least we have been together,

Don't bother trying to restrain each other, No verbal commitment is needed.

As long as we have had it, It's enough for you and me,

There are many memories in a person's life,

I only wish that you have me in your memories...

The celebration atmosphere was exceptionally warm. We sang "Ping Ju" with warmth, and the entire audience applauded. All 150 guests were in high spirits. Raising their wine glasses, they cheered, "Drink to win," elevating the atmosphere to its zenith. In doing so, they conveyed blessings and love to everyone present. At this point, the stage light no longer shone solely on me; everyone had their own spotlight.

Each person became the protagonist, for without them, there would be no birthday celebration.

Throughout the night, relatives and friends who hadn't seen each other for a long time greeted each other warmly, sharing life stories while savoring delicious food. Over the years, we had all experienced different ups and downs, but in that moment, we were reunited, feeling the warmth of friendship and family.

What made the night truly special was the continuous laughter and enjoyment shared by all. I felt incredibly fortunate to be surrounded by so much love and friendship. The 70th birthday celebration banquet became one of the most memorable moments of my life. I felt like the luckiest person in the world, having so many people who cared for me, a wonderful hometown, and relatives and friends accompanying me throughout my life.

The 70th birthday celebration banquet served as not only a reflection on the richness of my life but also the beginning of confidence and anticipation for the future. This birthday celebration will forever be cherished in my heart, becoming the highlight of my life.

With this birthday celebration, there will be a party to celebrate the 54th anniversary of the Miri Xieyuan Basketball Men's and Women's

Team in Sibu on July 17, 2023. Everything is thanks to the spirit of unity and friendship among a group of good sisters. Long live friendship! Everyone is also looking forward to next year, which marks the 2024 Miri Xieyuan Basketball Men's and Women's Team's 55th Anniversary Party! Let's raise a toast to enduring friendship! Cheers!

"Celebrating the 70th birthday, with happiness all around."

"At my 70th birthday party, I celebrated with family and friends.

Chapter 24
Climb Mountains and Challenge Your Limits

I feel that my life journey is like a mountain, full of dangers and challenges. I believe that the situations I face when climbing the mountain will mirror my life experiences. There will be unforeseen difficulties that will give me unparalleled feelings and experiences along the way. I am looking forward to the pleasure brought by the scenery, and it is because of this expectation that I feel ready to do it.

Some people say that 70 years of life are rare, but after experiencing countless ups and downs, I am still curious about the unknown world and want to explore the magic and beauty of nature. For decades, I have traveled around the world admiring the magnificent beauty of nature. When I was 71 years old, I decided to climb a high mountain to experience the condescending feeling. After this idea formed in my mind, I then had to choose the peak to climb among the many steep mountains.

But why choose to climb Mount Kinabalu? My husband is very supportive of my dreams. One day when we were watching a TV program, we happened to see a program introducing the highest peak in Southeast Asia, which is famous for its magnificent peaks and majesty - Mount Kinabalu in Sabah, Malaysia. The program also recommended that this mountain is worth climbing. A thought immediately came to my mind: It's her, it's her, the sacred mountain of Kota Kinabalu! A decision is often made in an instant.

However, due to heart health problems, my husband does not allow such strenuous exercise and cannot accompany me on this thrilling mountain trip.

From the very beginning, I knew that I was not a professional climber, and given my advanced age, it would not be easy to climb Mount Kota Kinabalu. It required not only physical strength and endurance but also spiritual determination and perseverance! So, after I decided to summit Mount Kota Kinabalu, I made detailed preparations starting from the next year and insisted on regular physical training. I ran 12 kilometers every day, carrying 10 pounds of weight, for 3 hours. When I have free time, I also ride a bicycle in my neighborhood to exercise my waist and legs. Over the past year, I have lost 7-8 kilograms. During the physical examination, the doctor also praised that my body function was better than before. In addition, I also actively learned about mountaineering knowledge, understood the climate, terrain, and climbing routes of the sacred mountain, and worked hard to prepare for difficulties.

Finally, the karma was sufficient, and I set off for the Holy Mountain of Kota Kinabalu on July 26, 2023. My nephew Shen Jian and I embarked on the arduous journey together with two experienced mountaineering leaders and tour guides hired.

Day 1: Departure and Preparation (July 26)

After the team leader picked us up at the hotel in downtown Kota Kinabalu, the group took a truck to Kundasang. We stopped at a grocery store on the way to replenish basic mountaineering supplies and then continued to the destination for about 3 hours. We stayed in the chalet at Poring Hot Springs. At about 10 o'clock that night, we listened to the team leader's report and packed our backpacks. Looking at the peaks towering into the clouds, I felt surges of emotion in my heart and said to myself, "Kota Kinabalu, I'm finally here! Just wait; I will peek into your heart."

Day 2: First Section of Mountain Climbing (July 27)

Today is overcast and a bit cloudy. At 6 o'clock in the morning, we got up early to prepare. I wore light hiking gear and checked the water and supplies in my backpack. I was full of anticipation and excitement. After breakfast and making sure everything was ready, we took the shuttle van and set off to Kinabalu Park HQ. Around 8:45 a.m., we registered at the Timpohon Gate checkpoint, the entrance to the mountain climb at an altitude of 1,860 meters, and began the ascent. The team leader stayed at the foot of the mountain waiting for us, while the mountain guide led us to the top.

From here, there are seven rest stops along the 6-kilometer climb up the trail stairs to Laban Rata Resthouse. Depending on your physical strength, it will take about 4-6 hours to reach your accommodation for the night. After passing through the Dingbohan Gate, approximately 10 minutes into the walk, I was pleasantly surprised to see Carson's Fall, with its gurgling sound and splashing water.

Continuing uphill, facing the seemingly endless road, I hung up my hiking permit, shouldered my hiking bag, held my hiking poles in both hands, cheered myself up, and started. Our team was arranged with my nephew in the front, me in the middle, and the mountain guide at the back.

In the first few hours, especially after passing the first and second rest stops (Kadis Shelter, 1981.7 meters above sea level, and Ubah Shelter, 2081.4 meters above sea level), I felt relaxed and in good physical condition. I chatted and laughed with my nephew and the mountain guide, and even took photos with my mobile phone. At this time, the terrain was full of vegetation, with pitcher plants and ferns visible everywhere. The road was also clearly marked. Every 0.5 kilometers, there was a sign indicating the altitude, and resting places were available every 500-1000 meters above sea level.

In my memory, the third rest stop is Lowii Shelter. Looking around, I could see bamboos, tree ferns, and mossy forests. Rhododendrons were also visible. Along the way, we encountered other climbers ascending the mountain. They asked us to help take pictures, and we had a lot of fun communicating with each other.

About 3 hours later, we had lunch at the fourth rest stop, Mempening Shelter, at an altitude of 2515 meters, and observed squirrels, tree shrews, and birds seemingly unafraid of humans. After lunch, we continued until the fifth rest stop, Layang-Layang Shelter, located at an altitude of 2702 meters. The soil on the trail turned orange, and the plants underwent dramatic changes. My nephew, the mountain guide, and I rested there, taking photos together with heart gestures.

As we continued to climb, the vegetation decreased, turning into shrubs, and the air became thinner. The steepness of the mountain road and the change in the plateau climate initially made it a bit difficult for me. When I arrived at the sixth rest stop (Villosa Shelter), I looked around and found well-maintained roads, sturdy ladder safety railings, and some difficult sections paved with wood. However, looking up, there were only endless steps that seemed to have no end. The forest was quiet, with tall trees covered in moss, leaves rustling in the wind, and occasional birds chirping. My heart felt calm, my mind was empty, and I concentrated on my journey.

I cheered myself up and soon arrived at the seventh rest stop (Paka Shelter). Around 5:50 pm, after a total of 9 hours, we finally reached the mid-level of Mount Kinabalu and stayed at the mountain house, the Laban Rata Guest House at an altitude of 3272 meters. Upon entering the restaurant, I noticed some hikers who had arrived early, resting and chatting inside. After our rest, we had a buffet in the restaurant, where I met new friends from around the world, sharing stories and dreams. After dinner, everyone quickly returned to their respective rooms to rest and replenish energy for tomorrow's summit attack.

Day Three: Summit and Return (July 28)

At 1 o'clock in the morning, the camp stirred with activity. We rose from our makeshift beds to partake in a midnight snack that would fuel us for the formidable journey ahead. Equipped with the essentials— windproof jackets, headlamps, hiking hats, sturdy boots, trekking poles, and waterproof covers—we initiated the final 2.5-kilometer ascent to the summit at approximately 2:40 in the morning. Our departure point was Laban Rata, and our destination, the pinnacle of Low's Peak, standing proudly at 4,095 meters above sea level.

The path was strewn with empty granites, and the mountain trail, rough and obscured in the pitch-black darkness, made it challenging to discern the route. We relied solely on the feeble illumination of our headlamps to pierce through the obscurity. The mountain wind blew relentlessly, causing an involuntary shiver with every step. Each stride felt burdensome, every breath is laborious.

The weather proved unkind. Around 3:20 in the morning, an unforgiving wind swept down from the mountain, accompanied by a bone-chilling temperature of minus 6 degrees. Thick fog descended like rain, saturating us and exacerbating the already arduous conditions. We encountered the zenith of difficulty, clinging to the ropes with a death grip, fearing a misstep would send us into the abyss. The mountain path, steep and demanding, required us to ascend one by one, each step demanding a monumental effort.

As the physical toll intensified, my legs ached, and my strength waned rapidly. Fearing I might hinder my nephew's progress, I urged him to forge ahead while I committed to catching up under the watchful eye of our mountain guide.

Summit hopefuls were mandated to reach the Sayat-sayat Check Point at 3,668 meters by 5:30 in the morning for summit registration. While my nephew successfully met the deadline and continued the ascent, I arrived 15 minutes tardy, finding the checkpoint closed. This regrettable delay dashed my hopes of completing the remaining 1.5

kilometers to the summit, at an elevation of 427 meters.

The Sayat-sayat Check Point, offering only basic amenities and a solitary toilet, became our temporary refuge. Deciding to await the break of dawn, we observed the challenging terrain ahead—hard, oddly shaped granite interspersed with tenacious shrubs and grass thriving in the crevices. The distant skyline teased the outline of the summit amid clouds and mist, hinting at the perilous rocks and cliffs awaiting those daring the final climb.

At 6 o'clock in the morning, we commenced our descent from Low's Peak back to Laban Rata. The journey downhill was formidable, featuring numerous rope-assisted sections where we descended slowly in single-file lines. My nephew, having reached the summit, returned later to join us. As the clock approached 8 a.m., clouds and fog materialized, hindering visibility for climbers on the descent.

Clad in lightweight clothing, we hastened our descent, indulged in a hurried breakfast, packed our belongings, checked out, and embarked on the grueling journey down the mountain. The fatigue, both physical and mental, weighed heavily on us. Having walked for over 10 hours since the previous day, with a mere 3 hours of sleep, we were utterly spent. The high-altitude environment induced dizziness and weariness, akin to altitude sickness. Every step down the seemingly endless stairs felt mechanical as if my legs and feet had lost control.

Three kilometers away from the Dingbohan gate, exhaustion took its toll, and I vomited at the Mempening Shelter. Recognizing the limits of my endurance, I persevered cautiously, prioritizing safety. Assisted by the mountain guide, I was carried down the mountain by a porter. Upon reaching the mountain's base, a semblance of relief washed over me, though more than 200 steps remained to ascend to the halfway house to retrieve my luggage.

By the time, we reached the Dingbohan Gate at 4 p.m., we had completed the descent. At 4:30 p.m., we arrived at the Kinabalu Park headquarters, where we received our mountaineering certificates. My nephew's certificate, vibrant with color, celebrated his triumphant summit, while mine, in black and white, recounted the challenges faced on the ascent.

Post-adventure, we indulged in a hearty dinner and spent the night in a wooden cabin at Poring Hot Springs. Although my quest to conquer the sacred mountain fell short of reaching the summit, the climb served as a profound physical and mental challenge, a spiritual purification, and a source of personal growth. Despite the capricious weather and treacherous mountain paths, I pressed forward, inch by inch, giving my best to the ascent.

In reflection, I reminded myself that time flows like water, but my enthusiasm and courage remain undiminished. As long as dreams reside in my heart, life holds boundless possibilities. With unwavering determination, I pledged to face future challenges with a youthful mindset, continuing to inscribe my tale of glory and pride on the journey of life.

"Climbing mountains and reaching new heights, challenging the limits."

"I took a photo with the team leader (center) at the headquarters of Kinabalu Park in Kota Kinabalu."

"My nephew and I are at the Timpohon Gate, the entrance to the mountain climb at an altitude of 1,860 meters, after registering at the checkpoint and preparing to start our ascent."

"I hold the trekking pole, taking one step at a time. "The footprints lead upward."

"During a break, I looked at the surrounding plants and experienced a completely different ecological landscape."

"The second rest station is located at 2081.4 meters, at Ubah Shelter. Here, you can find the rare Borneo pitcher plant – Nepenthes Lowii, so along the way, you can see some oddly shaped plants by the roadside." 。

"I continued until the fifth rest stop, located at an altitude of 2,702 meters."

"The trail markers are very clear along the way."

"I acted as the photographer, capturing moments for others."

"At Laban Rata's Layang-Layang Shelter, where the trail soil turned orange-yellow, my nephew and I took the opportunity to snap a photo together."

"I passed the sign marking an altitude of 2,445 meters."

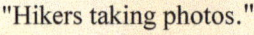

"Hikers taking photos."

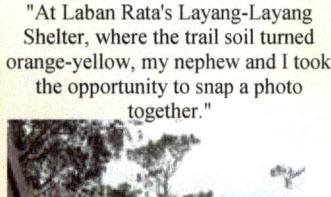

After passing the sixth rest stop, Villosa Shelter (elevation 2,690 meters), as I climbed along the trail, I was rewarded with a spectacular view of Mount Kinabalu towering into the clouds."

"I continued climbing upward, refusing to compromise!"

"Along the climb, I took in the ever-changing scenery along the way."

"Laban Rata Resthouse, located at an altitude of 3,272 meters, is the largest mountain lodge and also home to the restaurant."

"We stayed at a wooden chalet in Poring Hot Springs."

We finally reached the mountainside of Panalaban and took photos with climbers from all over the world. 。

"The entire climb of Mount Kinabalu requires a mountaineering permit, as well as a certificate upon completion of the climb."

"My nephew and I received our mountaineering certificates. The certificates are slightly different: my nephew's certificate is in color, as he successful reached the summit, while mine is black and white."

Chapter 25
Buddha Seeds Sprout in the Heart and Form Shades

When I immigrated to Canada in 1973, I chose to settle in beautiful Edmonton. The new life was full of hope and opportunities, but because of the trivialities of life, my inner peace was on the rocks. I was full of hesitation and helplessness about the unpredictable and foreseeable future. Standing in the face of a series of challenges in life, I needed a kind of spiritual inspiration, a strength to support me to move forward unswervingly; my desire was almost greedy.

As I searched and searched, my relationship with Buddhism matured. I met Vajra Master Lian Zhi (Liao Yunling) and began to understand the true Buddhist sect. In 1978, with good luck and the company of my love, I took my two daughters on a 1 hour and 40-minute flight from Edmonton to Vancouver and then drove 2 hours to Seattle, USA to meet the founder of the True Buddhist Sect, Lotus Living Buddha Lu Shengyan. My husband and I both received the refuge initiation from the living Buddha Lian Shengyan at his home and were given the Dharma names "Lian Fu" and "Lian Jie" respectively. During the conversion ceremony, I prayed for good health, that all my wishes would come true, for peace and joy. It seemed very simple, but it was very precious. Isn't that what people want in their lives? No matter how rich you are, a life of peace is not as good as peace of mind. And because of my prayers throughout my life, whenever I faced the lowest point in my life, I always felt like "there is a bright future in the dark, and I can survive from a desperate situation." This has always been my portrayal.

My husband and I took refuge in Living Buddha Lotus Shengyan and became disciples of the True Buddha Sect. We are each other's

Taoist companions. My Buddhist name is Lotus Buddha. The names of the True Buddha Sect often have hidden meanings. The first character of the names of all the disciples of the True Buddha Sect is "Lotus." "Lotus" comes out of the mud but remains unstained, and my word "Fu" means pure, fresh, and beautiful, implying auspicious and beautiful pure flowers. My life was lacking such positive energy, so this Dharma name came at the right time and started my spiritual journey.

In 1979, I bought the third house. The small house with the number 8122 became one of the temporary Buddhist halls for fellow practitioners of the True Buddha Sect in Edmonton at that time, and the temporary hall for the other two practitioners. The Buddhist halls were located in the homes of Liao Zhiqiang (now the eldest brother of the Vajra Master Lian Zhi) and Liang Yongming (the master Shi Lian Ping Vajra who is now a monk). Fellow disciples took turns practicing and having dinner in these three places, and it was a harmonious time until a businessman sponsored the venue. From then on, we had a fixed fellow practitioner in the Buddhist hall, and we would get together every week. In my heart, I felt that a Buddhist hall had been built where I lived because it was the gathering place of all virtues, the pure land of the heart, and a symbol of our union with the true Buddhist sect. Fellow disciples could learn and communicate together, and practice together. In this Buddhist hall, I felt the warmth of home and found spiritual sustenance.

Afterward, we felt that we should set up a monastery belonging to the True Buddha Sect in Edmonton so that the local True Buddha sect disciples could have a sense of belonging. With joint efforts, it took about 5 years from fundraising to building the church. During that time, Jingyin Hall was established, which later became the present Jingyin Lei Zang Temple. The majestic Jingyin Lei Zang Temple of the True Buddhism Sect is the spiritual refuge of the True Buddhism disciples in Edmonton.

I have also gone to Seattle, USA, twice to attend the Dharma meetings of the Living Buddha Lu Shengyan. Each time, I was filled with Dharma joy. The positive energy brought by the curling green smoke around the Buddhist temple was like nectar filling my dry heart, and my soul felt like it had a SPA.

I have been in two serious car accidents, and my life almost hung by a thread each time. But it was my religious beliefs and spiritual practice that allowed me to persevere and regain balance in my life.

However, another test came. The diagnosis of breast cancer was like a heavy blow, severely affecting both the body and the mind. The pressure caused by cancer is mostly mental. For me, this test is not regarded as the straw that broke the camel's back. Instead, I regard it as a lesson in life. I did not give up, persisted in reciting the mantra, chanting the Buddha's name, and practicing continuously. This perseverance became a source of strength. Drinking from the source of strength allowed me to overcome adversity. I also felt the Buddha's blessing from Living Buddha Lotus Shengyan, and the religious power allowed me to persevere. In each treatment and recovery, I feel that religion has always been a spiritual support in my heart. It gave me the strength to face the pain of treatment bravely and to maintain inner peace and strength.

On weekdays, I also worship Guanyin. There is a Buddha in my heart, and I recite the Buddha's name every day. I recite "Namo Amitabha" in my mind all the time. Will it be boring? Will it be tasteless? Won't! On the contrary, when you have distracting thoughts, just recite the Buddha's name, and your mind will be purified. This kind of feeling can only be understood but cannot be expressed in words. Only fellow practitioners know it!

Through religion, I learned perseverance, courage, love, and belief in the miracle of life. It taught me how to maintain inner peace in the face of difficulties and how to find relief in pain. It made me understand that no matter what happens, my soul has a refuge and a guide. It is my strong pillar in the ups and downs of life. It is not only a belief but also a part of my life, a spiritual support, a powerful force, a spiritual nourishment, and an eternal light.

I once used my own house as a place for fellow practitioners. It was from this origin that the True Buddha Sect became my spiritual home and inner harbor! It is also because of the origin of True Buddhism that I am also a Buddhist.

Chapter 26
Love in My Heart, Forever Remembering My Furry Child

Happiness came quietly on July 14, 2008, and the seeds of sadness were planted on this day, sprouting into towering trees on July 13, 2023. Although I had done some psychological preparation and prepared for her departure, I still couldn't bear it when the day came. I realized that I had underestimated her place in my heart. It hurt, it hurt so much. It makes me unable to breathe; every time I miss you, I can't breathe for a long time. If someone could see my heart, he would find that her shadow has been imprinted on my heart unknowingly, very deeply... No matter how many days have passed, if someone mentions "Lovely," I will still remember her. There will be heartache.

"Lovely" is my pet fur baby who is part Chihuahua and Pomeranian, also known as Pomeranian. She came into my life when I was undergoing treatment for the third stage of breast cancer. She spent her short li   accompanying me. When I needed comfort and companionship the most, she cured my loneliness and made me no longer lonely every night.

In the summer of 2008, I was diagnosed with stage 3 breast cancer. The news hit me like a hammer, and I felt the shadow of death hanging over me. At that time, I was sad and depressed and walked into a pet store and looked around. I caught my eye at first glance at "Lovely," who was born on July 14, 2008. She was just 6 weeks old at the time. I picked up this cute little guy. My heart was instantly moved by her innocence and innocence, so I took her home with me without hesitation. Unexpectedly, she stayed with me for 15 years, becoming my family and the light of my life!

When I decided to bring her home, I had no idea that this little being would become a huge force in my life. I named this small dog "Lovely," which means "beautiful," because it has the intelligence and liveliness of a Pomeranian and the cuteness and docility of a Chihuahua. When she first came to a strange environment, she was frightened and unable to adapt as a young child, and she wailed all night long. I know that puppies need careful care, so even if the pain tortures me, I still drag the sick body and guide her to eat, eat small and frequent meals, feed her regularly and quantitatively, and ensure that she provides sufficient drinking water. At the same time, I must also pay attention to her internal and external deworming, vaccinations, and other matters. Although my sick body is tired, I know that there is a little life that depends on me for survival, so I can only support her with all my energy to take care of her. Who knows if this will actually be beneficial to my condition? Taking care of my furry baby every day, walking, playing with her, and teaching her some tricks made me temporarily forget the pain and anxiety of cancer and gave me great spiritual healing, thus strengthening my confidence in defeating the disease.

After that, "Lovely" quickly integrated into my life. She was not only my pet but also my friend, companion, and loyal companion. During treatment, when I felt tired and anxious, she was always there for me, comforting me with her warm eyes and passionate licks. It seems to sense my emotions and always knows when I need companionship and when I need comfort. Her companionship is not only physical but also spiritual. Whenever I feel down, she will come close to me and gently lick my hand, as if to tell me: "Everything is going to be okay."

A year later, after I finally defeated the disease, "Lovely" became inseparable from me. Even when I went on a trip, I would take her on the plane with me, and after landing, she would stay at a local pet hotel. If it doesn't work, I will leave her to my son and daughter-in-law to take care of her or hire workers to come and take care of her.

"Lovely" has orange and white fur. Her eyeballs are protruding, and her big eyes are as cute as grape balls. She has a gentle temper and is not aggressive, so she can get close to anyone.

As time went on, the bond between Lovely and me grew deeper and deeper. We spent countless days and nights together, sharing every detail of our lives. Her existence makes my life more exciting and meaningful. No matter how much pain and discomfort I feel, just one look at her puts a smile on my face.

Fifteen years passed quickly, and in old age, "Lovely," who had not been neutered, developed pyometra. Since she fell ill, she became weaker and weaker. Every time I hold her furry body, feel her body temperature, and think of her accompanying me through the difficult treatment time, I feel very sad. She gradually lost her vitality and her breathing was heavy, but whenever I called, she would raise her eyelids in time to respond, rolling her two black eyes, looking at me with attachment like a child. That year, you accompanied me in my loneliness, and now I accompany her in her old age. Sometimes I can't help but ask myself, does she need me, or do I need her?

When she went to the hospital, the doctor thought that her health condition was not optimistic, and since she was an elderly dog, the surgery was very risky. However, if she was not treated, she would deteriorate to the point of organ failure. However, I always comfort myself, as long as I see her eyes still shining, I feel that everything is not that bad. But I understand that she is getting older, already a long time in a dog's lifespan, and her time is running out.

There is always a moment of farewell in life. On July 13, 2023, in my hometown of Miri, I received the bad news from my love that the old "Lovely" had quietly passed away. Tears overflowed, and I was choked and unable to speak. When I returned to my home in Canada, I could no longer see her sleeping silently, waiting for me at the door. When she saw me, she stood up quickly, wagging her tail, and warmly welcomed me home. Only her ashes were quietly placed on the table.

I feel a huge emptiness and loss after losing this family member who has been with me for 15 years. When I was sick, she walked with me, but when she died of a serious illness, I was not by her side. Every time I think about it, my eyes turn red, and I feel guilty and self-blame. I kept thinking painfully that if I could stay by her side to take care of her and accompany her when she was critically ill, and feed her water and food through a tube when she couldn't eat, I might be able to prolong her life. Life, maybe we could continue our fate for a few more years?

However, despite losing "Lovely," I know she will always remain in my heart. This deep feeling is a special emotional bond that is not limited by time and distance. She taught me the true meaning of loyalty, selflessness, and love. Although she has passed away, our story will always continue in my memory, and the deep relationship with the furry child will always be the most precious part of my life.

"Lovely," thank you; you will always be the burning and shining light in my life.

"Love in the heart, forever remembering the furry ones."

I'm sorry to hear about Lovely. Saying goodbye to a beloved pet can be incredibly difficult. It sounds like she had a special place in your heart, and that moment of holding her one last time must have been both emotional and poignant.

The young and healthy Lovely.

Lovely's companionship is indispensable in our lives.

Lovely has always been by my side.

Lovely likes to lie at the doorstep.

Sometimes, I also bring Lovely with me.

She fills my life with happiness. She fills my life with happiness. Go on a trip.

Chapter 27
Ecological Balcony; Good Times

After residing in Vancouver for a while, I returned to Edmonton and moved into the top-floor apartment, No. 808. This top floor is spacious, with a living area of 1,100 square feet and a balcony of 900 square feet.

Six years ago, a Canadian Goose couple happened upon my balcony, looking for an ideal spot to hatch their next generation. We observed quietly, fearing to disturb them. Sensing our friendliness, they found a home in a corner of the balcony.

Every year from March to May, the Geese couple chooses to build their nests on my balcony. Their nests are simple and cozy, with some dead grass and leaves on the outside forming a circle, and some of their down feathers on the inside. They ensure the nest is comfortable and warm while maintaining privacy.

This pair of wild geese love each other and often cuddle up together, preening each other's feathers. There are usually 4-7 eggs in the nest, which are white or light yellowish-white. The mother goose is responsible for incubating the eggs alone, while the father goose guards near the nest. The incubation period is 25-30 days, and the goose parents will take care of the chicks for 40-73 days.

On May 17, 2023, a group of fluffy little yellow dots, namely baby Geese, emerged from their shells. If you look closely at their backs, you can see gray-green feathers. Three days later, we carefully brought them from the balcony downstairs and let them leave with their parents. Later, we believed that they would migrate and fly south in autumn until we meet again next spring.

These Canadian Geese are larger birds with long, black heads and necks, and long white spots on their cheeks that extend behind their eyes like a white scarf. Their wings are wide and dark, their backs covered with gray-brown feathers, their chests and abdomen lighter in color, and their legs and flippers dark green, giving them a very elegant look. The males and females have similar feather colors, but the females are smaller. These adorable birds are a protected species.

Although they may show aggression towards creatures around them during their nurturing period, perhaps because we treat them as honored guests, they do not attack us and instead let me hold their adorable baby geese in my hand.

I felt the warm little body of the chick with my hands. In the beauty and sacredness of this moment, I seemed to be able to feel the infinite gift of life. This is not only the continuation of time but also the arrival of a miracle. In this moment of epiphany, I realized how precious life is, how pure and amazing it is. From the birth of one life to another, in endless reincarnations, we witness the magic and incredibleness of nature. I deeply feel that this is similar to the plant world on the balcony.

After the Goose family set off, I started planning the balcony gardening. Due to Canada's climate and seasons, I go all out on growing vegetables and flowers from May to September every year. If you have the opportunity to visit my balcony, you will be attracted by the small plantation. The plants there are vibrant and lush, like a relaxing journey for the soul. Tomatoes are ripening in the warm sunshine, sunflowers are smiling up at the sunshine, and bougainvillea is swaying lightly.

I will place sun-loving plants on the balcony where they are sufficient according to their characteristics. Delicate and delicate plants are less tolerant of UV rays, while flowers with dense petals and thick textures are better able to withstand the sun's rays. I pay close attention to the moisture status of the plants and ensure timely and appropriate watering.

Vegetables and fruit trees usually need full sun, such as tomatoes, broccoli, cauliflower, celery, potatoes, cucumbers, strawberries, etc., so I plant them in full sun. In summer, I choose to water in the early morning and evening to avoid high-temperature damage to the plants and ensure that water can penetrate into the roots of the flowers.

Fragrance vines, petunias, sunflowers, bougainvillea, forget-me-nots, etc. like plenty of light. They grow very lushly on my balcony, and they seem to be showing their beauty to the sun. Plants that prefer less light, such as hostas, spring plumes, peacock arrowroots, watercress greens, etc., are carefully placed in appropriate places to ensure that they too thrive.

I choose different plants for planting according to different seasons. Different flowers bloom in different seasons, bringing brilliant colors to the balcony all year round.

The process of planting is not only a hobby but also a journey of spiritual joy. Every green leaf and every flower on the balcony is like a small miracle that embellishes my daily life and allows me to find a moment of tranquility in this noisy world. You can lie down or sit on your balcony or courtyard, have a meal or read a book, and enjoy yourself leisurely.

In fact, every second in life is a tribute to life. The beauty of life lies in its diversity. Every living thing has its own unique existence and value. Animals, plants, and microorganisms together constitute this colorful dance of life. This world is full of endless possibilities, and every life is a wonderful thread in the interweaving of this universe. We become humbled and awed before the miracle of life. Whether it's a flower blooming or a bird soaring, life shows us its beauty and mystery in various forms.

We are part of the stage of life, and each individual has an irreplaceable role. Together we weave the story of life, and our choices and actions will affect the direction of this story. Therefore, let us face life with respect and gratitude for the beauty of this moment. Let us cherish every breath and feel every heartbeat, because the wonder of life is around us, waiting for us to discover and cherish it.

"Eco-friendly balcony, beautiful moments."

"The black goose mother is incubating eggs in the nest."

"I placed the adorable gosling in the palm of my hand, and the goose mother wasn't worried at all!"

" The fluffy black goslings hatched from their shells, lovingly cared for by their mother."

"All kinds of flowers are blooming in full splendor, competing in beauty and radiance, creating a vibrant scene of dazzling colors and a lively spring atmosphere."

"The sunflowers thrive and unfold their petals with vitality."

"The sunflowers thrive and unfold their petals with vitality."

"It has all kinds of vegetables and fruits, including tomatoes, broccoli, cauliflower, celery, cucumbers, peas, and snow peas, among others."

"The tomatoes, heavy with fruit."

"The cauliflower is ripe."

"The red, fragrant vine flowers are large and vibrant."

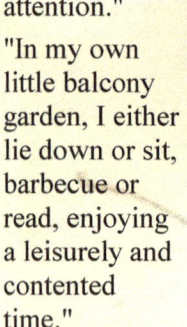

"Flowers of various colors bloom in a dazzling display, competing for attention."

白花酢浆草。

"In my own little balcony garden, I either lie down or sit, barbecue or read, enjoying a leisurely and contented time."

Chapter 28
Invincible Years; Flowers Bloom All the Way

In Bai Juyi's "Dan Ge Xing," a poem reflects, "Happiness cannot last long in life, and old age comes soon." It laments the fleeting nature of happiness and the swift arrival of old age. Having surpassed my sixtieth birthday and entered my twilight years, I resonate with this sentiment—such is life!

Reflecting on the first half of my life, it's a mix of joy and sorrow, sunshine and rain, blooming flowers and falling petals. Life's trivialities are mere spiritual pursuits, allowing the heart to follow its desires or vice versa.

As I look ahead to the next phase of life, there will be both deep and shallow steps, moments of sadness and joy, weariness and hope. I urge myself to embrace indifference and open-mindedness, to maintain tranquility and farsightedness. Witnessing the cyclical nature of life—flowers withering and blooming, clouds drifting—I aim to bathe in the spring breeze without arrogance, face adversity without harm, refine my character through correction, and broaden my mind through reflection.

In the twilight of life, while health permits, let me sing, echoing the sentiments expressed in Qi Long's "The Road of Life":

Looking back on this journey, Familiar yet strange it seems. Hesitation, tears, and laughter,

A wandering figure in my dreams.

This life, both short and long, Which inn awaits our meet? Sacrifices, hatred, and love,

What remains for oneself, so sweet?

Who comprehends life's solitude? Who unlocks its binding chains?

Who accompanies me on this journey? Who grasps life's ebb and flow with gains?

Understanding life's true happiness, Can anyone define this bliss?

Taking a moment for introspection, Navigating life's river, who am I to miss?

In life, we play multiple roles simultaneously. We are the children of our parents, the parents of our children, the loves of our partners, and the friends of our friends. Many times, in our dedication to playing these roles effectively, we unknowingly play a smaller role, losing ourselves in the process. Whether it's giving up a job for our children, sacrificing dreams for love, or setting aside personal pursuits for family obligations, one may wonder: when can we live for ourselves? Life offers only one chance, no TAKE 2. Living authentically and true to oneself is the key to embracing life without regrets.

Life has become more exhilarating since my retirement. Despite being over seventy years old, I've discovered that age is no impediment to pursuing new interests and hobbies. My love for travel, hiking, music, and writing has not only endured but flourished. Now, I can spread my wings and soar like an eagle, traversing mountains and ravines, flying overseas, gazing down at the Earth, and chasing the expansive blue sky!

Traveling has been an integral part of my life since my youth, offering fresh opportunities to explore the world. I have an ardent passion for savoring the cultural beauty of different countries and immersing myself in the customs of diverse places. I fondly recall closing our store every summer, embarking on month-long trips to various destinations, from Disneyland in the United States during my children's youth to spontaneous journeys across the United States, New Zealand, Australia, Vietnam, Thailand, Indonesia, China, and more in later years. On my 60th birthday, the entire family arranged a cruise, a memorable 15-day voyage from Auckland, New Zealand, to Sydney, Australia—from December 21, 2019, to January 4, 2020, a time when the global epidemic was in its early stages.

My love for nature extends to climbing mountains, pushing the limits, and feeling the Earth's pulse. Each ascent is a mental and physical exercise, traversing majestic mountains and wandering through serene forests, absorbing the wonders of nature. These experiences deepen my appreciation for every moment of life. To prepare for mountain climbing, I engage in daily walks of 12-24 kilometers, maintaining physical fitness.

Travel and climbing are not my sole passions—music holds a significant place in my heart. I commenced learning the cello in September 2023, fulfilling a long-standing desire. Inspired by my son's initial interest in the cello, I embarked on this musical journey to make up for the past. Despite the challenges of learning the cello at an older age, the instrument brings me immense joy. The rich and resonant tones create a sense of calm and contentment, enriching my spiritual world. Music, in all its forms, has become the sustenance of my soul.

As a classical music enthusiast, I frequently attend concerts and opera performances, immersing myself in the enchanting sounds. Each performance is a soul-refreshing experience, making me forget my age and rediscover the infinite possibilities of life. I firmly believe that the pursuit of beauty is timeless. My favorite singer, the renowned Hong Kong music producer Alan Tam, with his diverse repertoire, including "Love Must Have a Last Resort," "Friends," and "Silent Gratitude," captivates me with his exceptional singing ability.

In recent years, I've actively ventured into Chinese writing, dedicating substantial time to posting on Facebook Moments. To enhance my writing skills, I've read numerous books, embarking on a journey of self-learning and knowledge expansion. This newfound challenge fuels my passion, allowing me to express thoughts, and emotions, and share stories and insights with a broader audience.

Retirement hasn't halted my life; it's ushered in a new beginning, enabling me to embrace the essence of living for my dreams. I've realized that age is merely a number. By pursuing one's passions, maintaining a love for learning, and nurturing curiosity for life, one can naturally remain forever young. I eagerly anticipate each upcoming day filled with the joys of travel, music, and creative expression. I am invincible, with flowers blooming along the way!

"Timeless years, with flowers blooming along the way."

"As someone who loves to travel, I have left footprints in many countries."

"In my daily life, I go for a walk every other day, which lifts my spirits."。

"Sometimes, I ride my bicycle in my neighborhood to exercise my waist and legs."

"When the weather is clear, I almost go for a 12-24 kilometer walk every other day to exercise my body."

"I started learning the cello only after the age of 70."

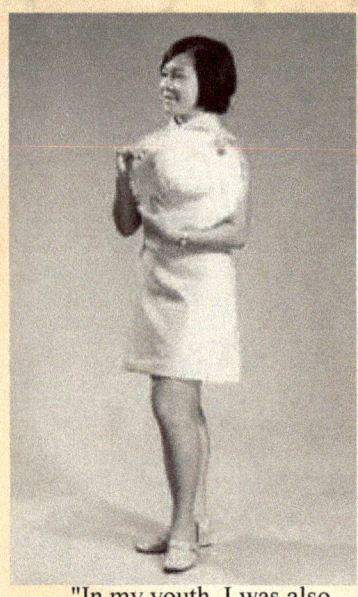

"At 70, one should still be full of confidence."

"In my youth, I was also graceful and charming."。

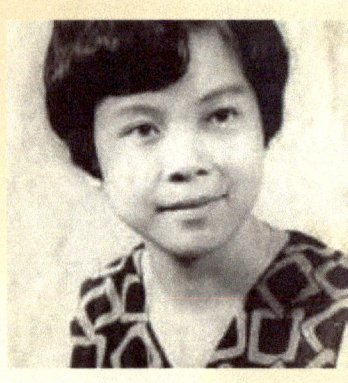

The me in my youth."。

"I, who love nature, formed an inseparable bond with the black goose mother."

Chapter 29
I Met a Better Version of Myself!

Embarking on the journey of writing an autobiography is like navigating the tumultuous waves of an inner transformation. From the calm reflection of a level lake to the stormy turbulence of a sea, the process is both surging and uneasy, filled with indescribable feelings. It's like a gentle breeze rustling through, softly stirring the silky willows. As stones are thrown into the lake, the ripples multiply, evolving into a seismic shift, creating a formidable tsunami that seems ready to engulf the narrator.

Within everyone's heart lies a small dark room, a repository for the most negative aspects of life. Usually left untouched, it's akin to a serene lake, mirroring the beauty of the surroundings. However, as the autobiography unfolds, the narrator is compelled to revisit the recesses of their life. Memories, whether good or bad, surge forth like water breaking through a dam. It's a constant knocking on the door of that dark room, aware that unleashing its contents might be akin to opening Pandora's box.

An autobiography is a moment when one's life is laid bare for a wide audience. It's akin to exposing one's soul, revealing it nakedly to the world—a profound unveiling, offering every bit of oneself without the ability to conceal. The book becomes a microcosm of the author's life, with every page representing a moment and every chapter a phase of growth and learning. The words on each page transcend mere ink; they carry unique stories, emotions, and experiences, inviting readers to touch the author's essence.

Throughout the process, the narrator experiences genuine laughter when recalling joyous moments and sheds real tears when revisiting sorrow. It's a fearless exploration of the depths of one's heart. Whether expressing happiness or sadness, the author writes unabashedly, engaging in a dialogue with the past and sharing their unique life experience with readers. There's no need for embellishments—only authenticity.

The narrator wonders about the reader's perspective. Will they relate to the story, finding echoes of their own experiences? Or will there be those who question the choices, decisions, setbacks, and achievements laid bare in the narrative? Regardless of the reader's reaction, the autobiography is a gift—an opportunity to connect, share, and perhaps inspire.

The hope is to convey positive energy through a genuine and resilient story—one filled with ups and downs, hardships, and growth. The autobiography is a brave attempt to express oneself, a means to establish a deeper connection with readers and etch one's life onto the pages of time.

Despite the unease, the narrator is willing to embark on this unknown journey, bravely opening up the past to illuminate it with the light of life between the lines. This is the real power of autobiography—an important step forward and an opportunity to face the past with courage. The narrator is willing to use words to write their story and share their life journey with readers—an endeavor to meet a better self!

Chapter 30
Conclusion: Unlock the Real Key to Life

Life is often described as a journey, an adventure into the unknown. In the quiet moments of the night, reflections on life play out like a videotape, revealing a series of doors—doors that hold doubts, regrets, potentials, and emotions. Each door stands as a formidable obstacle, yet every time the narrator summons the power and wisdom within, these challenges are met with the right keys. Life, then, becomes a series of doors waiting to be opened with the right mindset and the right keys.

Each person is born with a unique key—their talents, character, and experiences forming the intricate engravings of this key. Just as keys come in various materials and shapes, so too does each person's key have its own value and meaning. It may be finely carved metal, symbolizing talent and hard work, or rustic wood, representing simplicity and tenacity. The essence lies not just in possessing keys but in how one chooses to use them.

The real key to life is not only the keys one possesses but also how they are wielded. Life's doors are diverse, concealing opportunities and challenges behind them. Some doors require patience and perseverance to open, while others, seemingly easy to unlock, may reveal no treasure. The art lies in learning to choose the right doors and using one's keys wisely in life's journey.

Beyond the external doors, the true purpose of these life keys is to unlock the inner treasures within oneself. Emotions and potential, often hidden in the shadows, await discovery. The process of unlocking this inner treasure demands courage and determination. With each turn of the key, a deeper understanding of oneself emerges, drawing one closer to their authentic self. By facing fears and challenges, personal growth becomes a continuous journey towards strength and wisdom.

Crucially, the key to life is not solely for personal gain. It is also a tool to help others. Sharing knowledge, experiences, and emotions becomes an act of offering one's keys to help others unlock their doors to life. This sharing not only benefits others but also deepens connections and brings a sense of fulfillment and purpose.

"The Key to Life" is not a metaphor alone; it is a tangible reality in the narrator's life. It is an ongoing process, requiring self-reflection, learning, persistence, and adaptation. The belief in one's ability to find and use these keys is paramount. Each person possesses a unique key, and the key to a fulfilling life lies in continuously using these keys to open up new opportunities, challenges, and discoveries. As long as one remembers that the key to life is always at hand, they can move forward bravely, explore the unknown, unravel mysteries about themselves and the world, and open the door to their own life.

Addendum Chapter 31
Jump Into the Sky, Dare to Dream, and Fly.

In July 2024, I moved from Edmonton to Calgary, the city where my son lives. After settling in, I revisited my bucket list, one of the items being to try skydiving. During my climb of Mount Kinabalu in Sabah, I met a group of like-minded friends, and we agreed to go parachute jumping in Europe together. I was eager to fulfill this dream as soon as possible.

Now that I've moved to Calgary, I had the serendipitous pleasure of meeting my new friend, Uncle Bob, who is 92 years old. He is enthusiastic, energetic, and full of love for life and a passion for new challenges. At the time, he had just completed an extreme skydiving challenge! Uncle Bob's actions perfectly demonstrated to me that no matter what stage of life you are in, you can still chase your dreams and explore new possibilities.

When I accompanied him to the skydiving center and stood on the ground, looking up at the sky as I watched him gracefully glide to the ground, I was filled with admiration and emotion. After landing, he excitedly told me that this incredible flying experience couldn't be put into words and could only truly be understood through personal experience. His words touched me deeply and strengthened my determination to fulfill my desire to skydive and fully experience the extreme thrill of flying above the clouds.

So, I reached out to the local Skydive Extreme Calgary skydiving center to learn more about their services. The center, located just 45 minutes north of Calgary at Beiseker Municipal Airport, is the closest one to the city. I learned that the best time for skydiving is from May to September, as autumn weather makes skydiving less convenient due to the climate.

On August 25, 2024, a day with clear weather, moderate wind, and high cloud cover, I finally fulfilled this wish. The original skydiving date had been set for August 24, but it was postponed by one day due to bad weather.

On the day of the jump, my partner and son accompanied me to the skydiving center. We arrived at the center around noon and waited in the waiting room for the green light to signal that it was time to jump. However, the green light didn't come on, so we decided to have lunch while we waited. It wasn't until 4p.m. that the red light finally turned to green, and my skydiving adventure officially began!

Before the skydiving jump, I watched the safety video provided by the center and signed the "Tandem Skydiving Agreement." Later, under the guidance of the instructor, I put on my equipment and listened carefully to the skydiving process, essentials, and precautions. The instructor's professionalism and experience put me at ease. He would be doing a tandem skydive with me, where we would be connected by a harness and share a large parachute.

After boarding the plane, it took less than 10 minutes to reach an altitude of 12,000 feet. As the plane continued to climb, my excitement grew. Through the window, I could see white clouds cascading below, and the scenery was absolutely magnificent. There was a solo skydiver, two aerial photographers, myself, and the jump instructor, making a total of five people in the cabin.

Once we reached the predetermined altitude, the solo skydiver bravely jumped first, followed closely by an aerial photographer. When it was my turn, I carefully moved to the cabin door. The instructor nudged me once or twice, but nervousness and my fear of heights held me back. When he pushed me for the third time, we both jumped together, and another aerial photographer also leaped out of the plane with us!

While in the air, we were free-falling at about 120 mph for around 40 seconds. During this time, I experienced a strong sense of weightlessness as adrenaline surged through me. Although my mind went blank, I felt dizzy and even a little nauseated, I did my best to stay calm and focused. The wind roared in my ears, and my cheeks became numb from the intense gusts. Thankfully, my goggles allowed me to clearly see the spectacular scenery around me.

Two aerial photographers stayed with me throughout the entire process, communicating with gestures when necessary and recording every moment of the jump. From the moment they jumped out of the plane, they quickly adjusted their positions and stayed close to the instructor and me. The professional camera equipment they wore, along with the high-definition cameras on their helmets, captured our flight trajectory and every movement with stunning precision.

When the free fall reached a certain altitude, the instructor deployed the main parachute. The moment the canopy opened, my body slowed down significantly, and the tension gradually faded away. I finally settled into a peaceful, gliding state. At that moment, the scenery in front of me unfolded dramatically.

For the first time, I was looking down at the Earth from such a unique perspective, as if the entire world was stretching out beneath my feet.

From this bird's-eye view, the land appeared as a vast, intricate tapestry, with winding mountains and rivers, fields resembling patchwork green carpets, and roads snaking across the landscape like ribbons. The city buildings shimmered in the sunlight, arranged in perfect order, creating a serene and peaceful atmosphere.

The feeling of looking down at the world from such a high altitude was both awe-inspiring and calming, as if I were no longer a small being, but had become one with the vast world around me. I began to truly enjoy the sensation of soaring high in the sky. The sun shone brightly against the clear blue, the skyline seemed within reach, and my excitement grew with every passing moment.

The photographer continued to follow closely in the air, capturing shots of my instructor and me soaring through the blue sky from various angles. With each change of camera position, a new perspective emerged, showcasing the stunning scenery and the tranquility of the flight. In that moment, I almost forgot all my fear and nervousness, focusing solely on the boundless sky. My face radiated relaxation and joy, and the photographer skillfully captured every unforgettable moment.

Under the guidance of the instructor, we safely landed on a large grassland. The parachute slowly spread out on the ground, mirroring the calmness I felt the moment my feet touched the earth. My partner and son were already waiting at the landing site, capturing precious photos of the moment. After completing the skydive, I was also given a skydiving certificate of honor to forever commemorate my courage in jumping from an altitude of 12,000 feet.

Many people ask me, "Is tandem skydiving safe?" The answer is yes. Tandem skydiving is a highly safe experience, as it is accompanied and managed by professional instructors throughout the entire process— this includes parachute deployment, control, and landing. Skydivers only need to enjoy the thrill of flying at high altitudes. As long as participants are in good physical condition and do not have health issues such as acrophobia, high blood pressure, or heart disease, most people can take part in this exhilarating sport, with no age limit.

I was incredibly excited about this skydiving experience, but the whole process felt incredibly fast. From the moment I boarded the plane to when I landed, it took about 30 minutes. It seemed that as soon as I began to truly absorb the experience, it was already over in the blink of an eye. The freedom and thrill of flying was intoxicating.

It felt like a breathtaking fireworks display—vibrant and awe-inspiring. After the dazzling spectacle, all that remained was a beautiful memory and a touch of regret that it had ended so quickly.

So, I've already started planning my next skydive. This time, I hope to experience every moment more calmly: from the accelerated heartbeat as I jump out of the cabin door, to the lightning-fast sensation of freefall, to the peaceful glide after the parachute blooms. I look forward to re-experiencing the freedom and unrestrained joy of flying in the sky, and I want to more deeply feel the meaning and satisfaction of breaking through my own limits. The new, broader perspective from above fills me with gratitude for life, and I now cherish every inch of the land beneath my feet and every moment of my life.

If you've ever considered trying it, why not take this extraordinary step bravely?

MY LIFE JOURNEY

ARRANGED BY CHUA YONG CHEE

NARRATED BY BEE SIAN SIM

PUBLISHED IN 2025

ISBN 978-0-99-702549-

9 780997 025491